PABLO NERUDA

All Poets the Poet

by

Salvatore Bizzarro

The Scarecrow Press, Inc.
Metuchen, N.J. & London
1979

Frontispiece: Neruda in Isla Negra
photograph by Antonio Quintana Contreras,
used with permission

Library of Congress Cataloging in Publication Data

Bizzarro, Salvatore.
   Pablo Neruda : all poets the poet.

   Bibliography: p.
   Includes index.
   1. Neruda, Pablo, 1904-1973--Criticism and
interpretation.
PQ8097.N4Z584   861   78-24437
ISBN 0-8108-1189-8

El pueblo unido
jamás será vencido

To Salvador Allende
and to a free Chile

PREFACE

The purpose of this book is to analyze the social and political themes in the poetry of Pablo Neruda from 1936 to 1950 (Part I), and his later works in the context of the poet's total development (Part II). Books in English on Neruda's work are remarkably few and the present study is an effort to meet the deficiency in part. Since the publication of the Canto general in 1950, Neruda's reputation has steadily increased--as revealed in the growing number of isolated translations of his poems, in the publication of critical studies and appreciations, and in his receiving the Nobel Prize for Literature in 1971. But until now there has been no adequate attempt to present to the English-speaking world a cohesive survey of the poet's life and works.

The Introduction serves as a background to Neruda's early life and poetry, necessary to an understanding of his poetic evolution. Chapters I and II deal with the political conversion of the poet and with his new conception of art. "Reunión bajo las nuevas banderas," España en el corazón, and the poems dedicated to Stalingrad (which comprise the last three sections of Tercera residencia) introduce social and political themes in his poetry. Chapters III and IV analyze the "engaged poetry" of the Canto general, paying particular attention to "Alturas de Machu Picchu" (Chapter IV). Thus ends the first part, showing that Neruda's work was the result of two major events in his life: his witnessing of the Spanish Civil War and his adherence to the Communist Party. With the last three sections of Tercera residencia and with the Canto general, Neruda gives us a poetry whose foundations rest on the doctrine of social realism.

The second part of this study deals with his later works, not examining the form and content of individual poems but, rather, his poetry as a whole. Following his continuous search for a direct and simple expression of reality, Neruda's poetic techniques developed hand-in-hand with his thought. Chapter V analyzes his evolution toward a simpler form, taking into account his books of Odes, and his more personal poems found in Estravagario and Memorial de Isla Negra.   The poet finds correspondence to objects, vegetative life and human life.   He also contemplates the self and reveals his own spiritual biography.   A study of his Memoirs is the subject of Chapter VI.   The last two chapters include conversations with Delia del Carril, who remembers Neruda tenderly, and a summary of a taped interview with Matilde Urrutia, which recounts the last hours of the poet.

In my analysis, I have not been directly concerned with political attitudes, but instead with Neruda's evolution as a poet and his interpretation of reality.   I have set out his growth to maturity from the beginning--growth not only as a poet, but as a whole person.

A word about translations.   When it is possible to translate word for word and retain the essential poetic qualities of the original, the translator's toil is made easy. Neruda's poems, however, are delicate works of precision and I found that with certain poems it was more difficult to translate a word than a whole verse.   Alastair Reid has expressed the translator's dilemma most lucidly: "some poems survive ... to become poems in another language, but others refuse to live in any language but their own, in which case the translator can manage no more than a reproduction, an effigy, of the original. "   With most translations, of course, one is never satisfied.

ACKNOWLEDGMENTS

I would like to express my gratitude to the many people to whom I am indebted for the preparation of this book. Especially, I would like to thank Alastair Reid, for his inspiration and guidance; Suzanne Oboler, for transcribing and translating into English the interview I had with Matilde Urrutia on Neruda's death, and for convincing me to undertake the writing of this book; Roger Heacock, for his help on the last chapter; Nathaniel Tarn, for allowing me to use my own translation of a very difficult poem; Thomas Mauch, of Colorado College, for his editorial assistance; and Fernando Alegría, of Stanford University, for his advice.

I am grateful, too, to my students Sally Antweiler and Dan Dickison, for helping me with some translations of Neruda's poems; Anita Bernard, known as Bono, for providing the expertise in her line drawing of Pablo Neruda that she brings to all her work; and Mary Beth Cahill, Lisa Dillon and Theresa Gregor, of the secretarial pool, for their patience and cooperation. I also owe a deep debt of gratitude to Colorado College for a grant to go to Chile in 1975 to interview Matilde Urrutia and Delia del Carril.

Finally, a word of appreciation to Monica Schmidt de Hoyos, Arnoldo de Hoyos, Emilio Ellena, Enriqueta ("Queta") S. de Quintana, Hormiguita, and to my many other friends in Chile who helped make the preparation of this book such an enjoyable experience.

*   *   *

Losada, S. A. , Buenos Aires, 1958, 1961, 1962.   Published
by permission of New Directions Publishing Corporation,
publishers of Pablo Neruda's Residence on Earth, translated
by Donald Walsh.   All rights reserved.   Translations of
these selections appearing in the text are by Salvatore Bizzarro.

      Selections from Neruda's Confieso que he vivido: memo-
rias, copyright © 1974 by the Estate of Pablo Neruda, courtesy
Carmen Balcells Agency.   From Canto general I and II by Pablo
Neruda, © Editorial Losada, S. A. , Buenos Aires, 1955.
From Odas elementales by Pablo Neruda, © Editorial Losada,
1958.   From Nuevas odas elementales by Pablo Neruda, ©
Editorial Losada, 1963.   From Tercer libro de las odas by
Pablo Neruda, © Editorial Losada, 1957.   From Memorial
de Isla Negra by Pablo Neruda, © Editorial Losada, 1964.
From Veinte poemas de amor y una canción desesperada by
Pablo Neruda, Santiago de Chile, 1924.   Translated by Sal-
vatore Bizzarro.   English Language translation copyright ©
1979 by Farrar, Straus and Giroux, Inc.   Reprinted with
permission of Farrar, Straus and Giroux, Inc. , and Souvenir
Press, Ltd. , London.

      "Pido silencio/I Ask for Silence, " excerpted with the
permission of Farrar, Straus and Giroux, Inc. , from Extravagaria by Pablo Neruda, translated by Alastair Reid.   Translation copyright © 1969, 1970, 1972, 1974 by Alastair Reid.
Originally published as Estravagario, copyright © 1958 by
Editorial Losada, S. A. , Buenos Aires.

      "Muchos somos/We Are Many, " and excerpts from
"Testamento de otoño/Autumn Testament, " with the permission of Delacorte Press/Seymour Lawrence, from Selected
Poems by Pablo Neruda, edited by Nathaniel Tarn, excerpts
translated by Alastair Reid, published by Delacorte, 1973.

      Selections from Memorial de Isla Negra by Pablo
Neruda, © Editorial Losada, S. A. , Buenos Aires, 1964.
Translated by Ben Belitt in Five Decades: Poems 1925-1970,
with the permission of Grove Press, Inc.   Translations of
these selections appearing in the text are by Salvatore Bizzarro.

      An excerpt from the "Introduction" by Fernando
Alegría to The Elementary Odes of Pablo Neruda by Pablo
Neruda, translated by Carlos Lozano, © Las Américas Publishing Co. , 1961.   Reprinted with permission of the publishers.

Selections from The Heights of Macchu Picchu by Pablo Neruda, published in 1967 by Farrar, Straus and Giroux. Edition © by Jonathan Cape, Ltd., 1966, translated by Nathaniel Tarn. Originally published as "Alturas de Machu Picchu" in the Canto general I, © Editorial Losada, S. A., Buenos Aires, 1955. Translations of the selections appearing in the text are by Salvatore Bizzarro, with the permission of Jonathan Cape Ltd., representing the Estate of Pablo Neruda.

*   *   *

A special thanks to Delia del Carril, Emilio Ellena, Enriqueta S. de Quintana, Bob Borowicz, in Chile, and Sara Facio, in Argentina, for the wonderful photographs they made available for this book.

CONTENTS

INTRODUCTION

The poetry of Pablo Neruda begins, as it ends, with the poet's fascination with nature. But it also reveals the recurrent, even obsessive imagery, the consistent underlying themes, which weld apparently disparate volumes of poetry into a kind of spiritual autobiography, into a testament of a man's struggle for existence, into a concern for the social and political realities of South America and its people.

The first part of this study proposes to analyze the social and political themes in the poetry of Pablo Neruda, attempting to show that from 1936 on it would be impossible to undertake an appreciation of his works criticizing them solely in aesthetic terms. With Tercera residencia, a collection of poems written between 1934 and 1943, and the Canto general, one of his major compositions, published in 1950, Neruda's poetry underwent a profound change, and so did his conception of poetic art. The purpose of Part I is to discuss the change from a historico-literary perspective, and to determine why the poet shifted toward a commitment to a political ideology and to social realism. Part II concentrates on the later works in the context of the poet's total development.

During the period from 1936 to 1950, Neruda's poetry was written under the stress of ideological conflict and political crisis. The poet believed that the work of art and the statement of thought--when these are responsible human actions, rooted in human need--are inseparable from historical and political context. He argued that there are books which are important at a certain moment in history, but once these books have resolved the problems they deal with they carry in them their own oblivion. Neruda felt that the belief that one could write solely for eternity was romantic posturing. It is ironic that the first two books of Residencia en la tierra--which Neruda has repudiated, not out of political fear, but because he genuinely believed that they misinter-

1

preted fundamental notions of social realism--should endure
among the most famous of his achievements.

The social themes in Neruda's poetry appeared as
early as 1923, in Crepusculario. In poems such as "Barrio
sin luz, " or "El ciego de la panderata, " the social message
is bitter and pessimistic: sordid descriptions of Latin American cities, a decadent social order, a bleak vision of the
future. No solution is offered for injustice and misery.
These early writings do not reflect a clear and convincing
ideology and the poet does not try to identify himself with
the people, as he does later on, in order to write a poetry
which could improve their conditions.

By the time Neruda became a member of the Communist Party and associated himself with the proletariat, the
social themes in his poetry had already taken on political
implications. Marxism gave him a clear ideology to follow
in order to bring about a new society in Chile and in the
world. This ideology was reflected in a class struggle that
would result in the fall of capitalism and would establish a
social organization that advocated the control and ownership
of industry, capital, and land by the community as a whole.
From 1936, when the Spanish Civil War began, to 1950,
when he received the Stalin Peace Prize for literature, the
social themes in his poetry became interrelated with the political themes in an attempt to transform society according
to what Karl Marx had prescribed. His poetry became less
bitter and, in solidarity with the fighting masses, Neruda
saw hope in the future.

Before we examine in detail the social and political
themes in Neruda's poetry written between 1936 and 1950,
and his work as a whole, we shall begin with a brief discussion of his early life and of the literary traditions that ex-
isted in Hispanic America. Such a discussion will be useful
in tracing Neruda's poetic evolution.

Ricardo Neftalí Reyes Basoalto (Pablo Neruda) was
born in Parral, in southern Chile, on the 12th of July, 1904.
Shortly afterwards, his family moved to nearby Temuco, a
small town with wooden houses and dirt roads that in winter
turned into mud because of the incessant rains. Vegetation
covered a good part of the surroundings with thick foliage,
and storms came from the sea. Distant erupting volcanoes
were a threat to the inhabitants. Outside of heavy rainfalls
and frequent inundations, fires and earthquakes were the most
feared calamities.

The lost world of childhood experience played a crucial part in the work of Neruda, who derived much of his
poetic originality from his attempt to interpret adult life in
terms of a permanent symbolism established in childhood.
Nature left a profound impression on the child and became a
symbol of creation, on the one hand, and of the destructive
force of the elements, on the other:

> Facing my house, the austral waters dug
> profound ruts, swamps of mourning clay,
> that in summer became yellow atmosphere
> through which carts creaked and wept
> pregnant with nine months of wheat.

> Frente a mi casa el agua austral cavaba
> hondas derrotas, ciénagas de arcillas enlutadas,
> que en el verano eran atmósfera amarilla
> por donde las carretas crujían y lloraban
> embarazadas con nueve meses de trigo [OC 648]. [1*]

All the joy and fears of growing up were experienced
by Neruda as part of a vast kingdom of plant life, with incessant winds and torrential rains; and so, it is not surprising that Temuco, the last fortress of the Araucanian Indians,
became the focus for most childhood memories, his symbol
for the whole of life, the essential setting for his poetic
creation:

> The first things I saw were trees,
> ravines decorated with flowers of wild beauty,
> humid earth, forests that lit up, and
> winter behind the world, unrestrained.
> My childhood is wet shoes, broken
> branches fallen in the jungle, devoured by lianas
> and scarabs, sweet days upon the oats, and
> my father's golden beard leaving
> towards the imposing majesty of the railroads.

---

*Notes begin on page 167. The simple designation "OC"
means Neruda's Obras completas, second edition, and will be
used throughout the text, with page number(s) added. Toward the end of Chapter Five, the fourth edition is cited several times, always as "OC4th." All the English translations
of Neruda's poetry will appear preceding the Spanish in the
text and are the author's unless otherwise indicated.

> Lo primero que vi fueron
> árboles, barrancas
> decoradas con flores de salvaje hermosura,
> húmedo territorio, bosques que se incendiaban
> y el invierno detrás del mundo, desbordado.
> Mi infancia son zapatos majados, troncos rotos
> caídos en la selva, devorados por lianas
> y escarabajos, dulces días sobre la avena,
> y la barba dorada de mi padre saliendo
> hacia la majestad de los ferrocarriles [OC 648].

Neruda lost his mother a month after he was born. His father remarried and the child was fortunate to have a kind stepmother whom he associated with poetry:

> Motherly love and poetry turned out to be for him almost identical, a consolation in life, a refuge, and a condition of tenderness. [2]

Of his stepmother he says: "She was diligent and sweet, had the sense of humor of peasants, and was affectionate and kind. "[3]

His father also played a significant role during the formative years of the youth. He was the hero of the exterior reality, the railroad man who guided his trains through the forests and smelled of burned coal. Neruda's references to his father, no matter what emotional coloring they are given, have one thing in common: they always convey a sense of awesome, godlike power. His father was the man who made the trains run, who established the law of the household and enforced it, who did not want his son to become a poet.

Neruda grew up in a frame house, where literature was a heterogeneous mixture of modern classics and adventure stories. The poet "reads the adventures of Buffalo Bill, and loses himself in the narrative of Jules Verne, Vargas Vila, Strindberg, Máximo Gorki, Felipe Trigo, Diderot, and Victor Hugo. "[4] But what was missing in his childhood experience, and consequently from his poetry, was religion:

> Only as a child of twelve did he visit a church with his stepmother; it was covered with moss and the absence of men was absolute. What remained engraved in Neruda's memory were the lilies outside, with their intense perfume. [5]

School became associated in the mind of the child with bitter cold.   Just like his house, the school he attended was built with freshly-cut wood, and just like his house, where he and his stepmother shivered with cold, the building was humid and without heat.   But it was there that Neruda had the good fortune of having as teacher a dark-haired woman who had come from Vicuña (northern Chile).   She lent him many books and encouraged him to read.   She became known to the world as Gabriela Mistral. 6

The evocation of landscape and climate in Southern Chile is everywhere apparent in Neruda's poetry.   In Anillos, written in 1926, the poet describes a typical day in winter:

Oh frightful winter full of swelling waters,
when mother and I were shivering in the furious
wind.   Rain falling from all directions; oh
sad and inexaustible squanderer.   The trains
lost in the forest howled and cried.   The wind
jolting, shook windows, knocked down fences;
desperate and violent, it deserted toward the sea.

Ah pavoroso invierno de las crecidas, cuando
la madre y yo temblábamos en el viento
frenético.   Lluvia caída de todas partes,
oh triste prodigadora inagotable.   Aullaban,
lloraban los trenes perdidos en el bosque.
El viento a caballazos, saltaba las ventanas,
tumbaba los cercos; desesperado, violento,
desertaba hacia el mar [OC 133].

And 12 years later, the occasion of his father's death brings back memories of the rainy South:

But everything can be explained, this tragic water was rain, perhaps the rainfall of just one day, of one hour, typical of our southern winter, rain water which had invaded roof tops and banisters, tiles and other materials and other bodies to arrive at the tomb of my dead kinsman.   Now, then, this awesome rain sprung from an impossible, inscrutable, extraordinary hiding place in order to reveal its torrential secret, showed me, with its mysterious pouring, my interminable connection with a determined life, region and death.

Pero todo se explica, esta agua trágica era lluvia, lluvia tal vez de un solo día, de una sola hora tal vez de nues-

tro austral invierno, y esta lluvia había atravesado techo
y balaustradas, ladrillos y otros materiales y otros muertos hasta llegar a la tumba de mi deudo. Ahora, bien,
esta agua terrible, esta agua salida de un imposible, insondable, extraordinario escondite, para mostrarme a mí
su torrencial secreto, esta agua original y temible me
advertía otra vez con su misterioso derrame mi conexión
interminable con una determinada vida, región y muerte. [7]

Again and again Neruda will use nature and its elements to
create his poetic world and will turn to the loneliness experienced in childhood and to the desolate rains of Temuco to
give us the most poignant images of solitude and anguish,
frustrated love and death. This squalid region of southern
Chile, where the poet spent the first 17 years of his life, is
easily recognizable in his later poetry which deals with social
and political themes, such as we find in "El fugitivo," or in
"Yo soy. "

    In 1926 Neruda went to study French at the University
of Chile, in Santiago, leaving behind the province and its way
of life. He found that in the Chilean capital the predominant
literary trends had begun during the last two decades of the
nineteenth century and were to continue until the 1930's. They
became known as Modernismo, which owed much of its innovations to a synthesis of the theories of the French Parnassian
and Symbolist poets; Post-modernismo, made up of "a generation of writers born between 1880 and 1896, which gradually
drew away from the ideals and practices of the modernistas"[8];
and Vanguardismo, a period which began at the conclusion of
the First World War and ended around 1930, and in which
various experimentations in poetry were made. As we shall
see, Neruda did not escape the influence of this millieu. Later, he began embracing the most advanced techniques of the
vanguardistas, using images that became more and more surrealistic and which made many of the poems of Residencia en
la tierra I and II obscure to the casual reader ("El reloj caído en el mar" and "Arte poética," among others).

    Neruda published his first book La Canción de la fies-
ta, in 1921, when he was 17 years old, and his second, Crepusculario, two years later. He had written them when he
was 15 and 17. At first he gives us sonnets, which are a
conscious imitation of the modernistas but which already show
deep feelings and originality of images: bread mixed with
rain, the perfume of the lilies in the field, the description of
the beloved made up of "body and dream" (carne y sueño).

In Canción de la fiesta, the poet uses one image--not a series
of them as he does in his later books--to describe one situation: "Men with a vibrant and sonorous laughter/ are the ones
who bring merrymaking in their arms" ("Hombres de risa vi-
brante y sonora/ son los que traen la fiesta en los brazos").
For its tone, vocabulary, and rhythm--the anapaestic hendecasyllable verse--the book is strictly modernista. [9]

    In Crepusculario, Neruda's typical lexical combinations
begin to take shape: penetrating stars, nocturnal silence, experience of nothingness, obsession, turbulent skies, torrential
rainfalls. The rain and the sea, with their incessant movement (building up and destroying at the same time), are present. The book uses the same form of the modernistas: the
alexandrine verse, the hendecasyllable sonnet, stanzas with
four and two lines, but the tone is post-modernista, approaching the social in poems such as "Barrio sin luz," and an "ex-
alted Romanticism" in poems such as those grouped under
"Pelleas y Melisanda."

    For Neruda, this conscious imitation of "other voices"
was essential. The Uruguayan poet Carlos Sabat Ercasty was
one of his models during this period of apprenticeship. The
influence of other modernistas can be detected in these youth-
ful books and is admitted by Neruda:

    I understand, friends, I understand it all.
    Other voices gathered with mine.
    As if I wanted to fly and the wings of birds
    came to my help, these foreign words came
    to unrestrain my dark inebriated soul.

    Yo lo comprendo, amigos, yo lo comprendo todo.
    Se mezclaron voces ajenas a las mías.
    Como si yo quisiera volar y a mí llegaran
    en ayuda las alas de las aves,
    así vinieron estas palabras extranjeras
    a desatar la oscura ebriedad de mi alma [OC 72].

Thus ends the book Crepusculario. In it, we can already see
the future poetry with social and political orientation. For
example, in "Maestranzas de noche," a preoccupation with the
working man is already present in Neruda. And it is for this
reason that this poem heads the collection Poesía política,
published in 1953.

    Neruda's third book, El hondero entusiasta, was begun

in 1932 but not published for another ten years.   Carlos Sabat Ercasty was his model once again.   Neruda, explaining
the influence that the Libro de amor had on his book, published it "as evidence of his ardent and excessive youth"
(OC 12).

These early writings have a certain elegance and polish, but they all share a central weakness: they do not express authentic personal experience in a convincing way, nor
do they create a landscape that is the poet's own.

Neruda showed such an original landscape in Veinte
poemas de amor y una canción desesperada, which he published in 1925.   But the novelty of the Veinte poemas did not
rest in the structure; the alexandrine verse, the stanzas with
four and two lines, and the free verse already used in Crepusculario were present.   Rather, it consisted in the images
and in the erotic theme, which had never been expressed in
South America, nor in Spain for that matter, with such a
force:

> Body of a woman, white hills, white thighs,
> you resemble the world, as you lie in surrender.
> My rough peasant's body seeds you
> and makes an offspring leap from the bottom of
>   the earth.
>   . . .
> But the hour of vengeance falls, and I love you.
> Body of skin, of moss, of avid and firm milk,
> Oh the goblets of the breasts!   Oh the
>   absent eyes!
>
> Cuerpo de mujer, blancas colinas, muslos blancos
> te pareces al mundo en tu actitud de entrega,
> Mi cuerpo de labriego salvaje te socava,
> y hace saltar el hijo del fondo de la tierra.
>   . . .
> Pero cae la hora de la venganza y te amo.
> Cuerpo de piel, de musgo, de leche ávida y firme.
> Ah los vasos del pecho!   Ah los ojos de ausencia!
> Ah las rosas del pubis!   Ah tu voz lenta
>   y triste! [OC 77].

In this book, Neruda abandons the easy comparisons
usually expressed with a simile.   He uses, instead, images
that have meaning by themselves.   He says, "white hills"
in order to qualify "body of a woman."

In Tentativa del hombre infinito, published in the same year, which reminds us of Tzara's L'Homme approximatif because of its long series of associated images, Neruda's models are the French Surrealists. But his poetry is more personal and there occurs a break with the past and tradition: free verse, free syntax, free orthography. Words become more forceful and images lose their logical meaning. In this chaos Neruda reveals his interior state. We are confronted with a poetry of transition that abandons the modernista and post-modernista modalities to adopt the poetic creed of the vanguardistas, using a language void of logic to represent an equally illogical reality. This poetry will become more hermetic with the publications of Residencia en la tierra I and II.

In 1927, after the publication of two works of prose, El habitante y su esperanza, and Anillos (the latter written in collaboration with his friend Tomás Lago), Neruda was recognized as an influential Chilean writer. He was offered a consular post in the Far East, which marked the beginning of his ten-year diplomatic career. He spent the next five years in India and Indo-China. His next two assignments as a diplomat took him to Argentina and Spain. In Buenos Aires, he met Federico García Lorca; in Madrid, he met, among others, the poets Rafael Alberti, Jorge Guillén, Dámaso Alonso, and Pedro Salinas. During his stay in Spain he also met Manuel Altolaguirre, with whom he founded the literary review Caballo Verde para la Poesía.[10] Neruda remained in Spain until shortly after the beginning of the Spanish Civil War. The years in the Orient contributed to an increase in the feelings of solitude which the poet had experienced as a child. The years spent in Madrid were of crucial importance to the change of orientation in his work.

By 1936 Neruda had already published Residencia en la tierra I and II (which covered the periods 1925-31 and 1931-35). These two books were published in Chile first, when Guillermo de Torre refused to publish them in Madrid, and then in the Spanish capital, through the efforts of Alberti. Soon after their publication, they became widely acclaimed in the Hispanic world, and Neruda's name figured prominently with that of García Lorca and other renowned poets of the so-called "Generation of 1927." The themes of these last two books were anguish, solitude and death, all expressed in an absurd world. Symbols and metaphors were used abundantly by the poet in this hermetic stage of his writings.

In Neruda's verse there is a continuous movement

which appears to represent the primordial chaos of the creation of the world.   His poetry, which concentrates exclusively on the overpowering elements of nature, is caught between water, fire, winds, in what seems to be the total disintegration of the universe.   Things in a state of decomposition surround the poet, who tries to convey in the most exact way the feelings that lie within him.   Neruda expresses himself in a surrealist manner, moving predominantly in the realm of dreams and the subconscious:

> His poetic method seems to depend on a magnetic force which draws elements from the surrounding reality.   It accumulates them and rolls them like the thread of a reel.   The poem grows and is strengthened: the material is absorbed in the rotary process, is compressed, and becomes a unified whole.   Nevertheless, this material seems to be disparate and heterogeneous, gathered accidentally, and at times savagely crude.   What makes it part of the poem is the emotional intensity underlying its arrangement.

> Su método poético parece depender de una fuerza de attracción, que coge elementos de la realidad circundante: los amontona en capas o los enrolla como el hilo de un carrete.   El poema crece, se vuelve más grande y más solido: el material es absorbido en el proceso rotatorio, comprimido, forma un todo inseparable.   Sin embargo, este material parece ser heterogéneo y disparatado, cogido accidentalmente, a menudo brutalmente crudo.   Lo que lo une a un poema es la fuerza del sentimiento, la intensidad en el curso poético. [11]

In the poem "Unidad" Neruda feels surrounded by disparate and most diverse things:

> Only one thing surrounds me, a single movement:
> the weight of mineral, the glow of skin
> become one with the sound of the word 'night':
> the color of wheat, of ivory, of weeping,
> old, discolored, uniform things
> made of leather, wood, wool,
> close in on me like walls.

> Me rodea una misma cosa, un mismo movimiento:
> el peso del mineral, la luz de la piel,

se pegan al sonido de la palabra noche:
la tinta del trigo, del marfil, del llanto,
las cosas de cuero, de madera, de lana,
envejecidas, desteñidas, uniformes
se unen en torno a mí como paredes [OC 164].

What unites all these things is precisely the unique existence
of each of them, and the fact that all of them participate in
the same movement which is responsible for their disintegration.

In the first stanza of the poem, reality is found in a
stone:

There is something dense, uniform, in the
        depth of being,
monotously repeating its number, its signal.
How easily noticeable that stones have
        touched time,
in their fine matter there is the smell of age
and of water brought from the sea, of salt
        and dream.

Hay algo denso, unido, sentado en el fondo,
repitiendo su número, su señal idéntica.
Como se nota que las piedras han tocado
        el tiempo,
en su fina materia hay olor a edad
y el agua que trae el mar, de sal y sueño [OC 165].

In the stone there are many years and generations. All existence rotates and can be seen through this one thing. The
enumeration of disparate objects, such as "things of leather,
of wood, of wool, / old, discolored, uniform, " includes symbolically all the other things that have not been mentioned,
even their opposites. Just as the stone represents all of
reality, the poet represents the center of this reality--yet
one who is outside of it and can perceive it (if he were whol-
ly contained by it, he would also have been contained in the
stone, in matter, in a non-transcendental state):

I labor silently, circling around myself
like the black crow upon death.
Central, isolated in the extremity of
        the seasons,
I meditate encompassed by a silent landscape:
a pleasant temperature falls from the sky,

an excessive empire of confused entities
draws itself together, encircling me.

Trabajo sordamente, girando sobre mí mismo,
como el cuervo sobre la muerte, el cuervo
   de luto.
Pienso, aislado en lo extremo de
   las estaciones,
central, rodeado de geografía silenciosa:
una temperature parcial cae del cielo,
un extremo imperio de confusas unidades
se reúne rodeándome [OC 165].

In "Entierro en el este" Neruda depicts death with
images that are disconcerting to the reader: a man destroyed by fire is reduced simply to "a dissolved breath,"
"a heady spirit," "a trembling ash" (un aliento desaparecido,
un licor extremo, una trémula ceniza) that falls upon the water.   The impressionistic description of a burning leg and
foot, or of contagious diseases that consume the body make
the reader meditate on the uncertain future of mankind.

In "Sólo la muerte" the poet describes death as a
needle looking for thread, or as "the tongue of death looking
for dead people." It appears everywhere:

Death lies in our bedsteads:
in the slow mattresses, in the black blankets,
lives stretched out and suddenly blows:
blows an obscure sound which makes the linen swell,
and there are beds sailing into harbors
where she waits dressed as an admiral.

La muerte está en los catres:
en los colchones lentos, en las frazadas negras
vive tendida de repente y sopla:
sopla un sonido oscuro que hincha sábanas,
y hay camas navegando a un puerto
en donde está esperando vestida de almirante
   [OC 200].

Treating this theme, Neruda does not present death to
us as the reality which will free man of life's burden.   For
the poet, death is insidious and sneaks up on man from everywhere.   Moreover, it represents man's contact with nothingness, with eternal darkness.

Emir Rodríguez Monegal sees the two volumes of Residencia en la tierra as parts of the same whole.[12] This is
true insofar as we are dealing with style. In spite of the essential unity of the books, however, we can also note a dif-
ference: in the first Residencia ... the poet seems more interested in milieu and the world in a state of disintegration;
in the second, on the other hand, the poet's main preoccupation is an eschatological one. Death is present in Residencia
en la tierra II. Man changes, loses the prime qualities of
life, and heads towards nothingness.

Reading poems from these two collections, we can see
the difficulty in interpreting some of them because of the
poet's arbitrary use of verbs and adjectives in an increasingly
irregular syntax. "Arte Poética," with its chaotic enumeration
of images, its juxtaposition of terms and symbols, is an illus-
tration of this[13]:

Oh, for each invisible drop of water I
        drink drowsily,
and for each noise I harbor, trembling,
I nurse the same absent thirst and the same
        icy fever,
a sound being born, a devious anguish:
as if thieves or ghosts were approaching,
in a fixed and deeply enveloping shell,
like a humiliated servant, a raucous bell,
an old mirror, or an abandoned house with
its solitary smell--where the guests file in
at night hopelessly drunk--and there is
a stench of clothes thrown on the floor
and an absence of flowers ...

Ay, para cada agua invisible que bebo
        soñolientamenta
y de todo sonido que acojo temblando,
tengo la misma sed ausente y la misma fiebre fría,
un oído que nace, una augustia indirecta,
como si llegaran ladrones o fantasmas,
en una cáscara de extensión fija y profunda,
como un camarero humillado, como una campana un
        poco ronca,
como un espejo viejo, como un olor de casa sola
en la que los huéspedes entran de noche
        perdidamente ebrios,
y hay olor de ropa tirada al suelo, y una
        ausencia de flores ... [OC 132].

Giving us a cluster of independent images, and a series of unconnected comparisons, Neruda depicts the anguish that torments him. To understand his message, we must keep in mind that the poet does not use a symbol to establish a direct relationship between the level of the real and that of the imaginary. Instead, he eliminates the real and makes the symbol stand, by itself, in the place of the reality it has annulled. The poet has the same "absent thirst" and "icy fever" for "each invisible drop of water" that he drinks. The adjectives "absent, icy, invisible" destroy the real meaning of the nouns they modify. Therefore we must look at the reality these symbols represent to clarify the meaning of these verses. The invisible water, while losing its material appearance, acquires a new meaning. It stands for all waters, whether they be visible or invisible. It becomes a metaphorical water that the poet drinks metaphorically. It becomes the symbol of all reality. The "absent thirst" expresses the poet's eagerness to capture this reality and interpret it in a poetic way. The "icy fever" reinforces the previous image since thirst and fever, usually occurring simultaneously, are placed in opposition to each other. The identification of a symbol with some aspect of reality that is not explicitly expressed, or of a term of a comparison with another term that is absent, destroys the traditional image with its mechanical associations to give us a poetry that is generally more difficult to interpret.

The pessimistic view of the world, which characterizes the poetry of Residencia en la tierra I and II was continued by Neruda in the first two sections of Tercera residencia, but ends with the last poem of "Las furias y las penas" (Section II). From this point on, a new phase in the evolution of Neruda's writings began. The poet would attempt to be less hermetic in his expression and to write a less metaphorical poetry for a larger number of readers.

Section III of Tercera residencia represents the political conversion of Pablo Neruda. His social themes now began to offer a solution to injustice and misery. The poet abandoned the contemplation of the self in a chaotic world and began to see order in things. His preoccupation was no longer with death but with life. He was willing to put his art at the service of social realism, being concerned primarily with the rights of his fellow men. From 1936 to 1950, Neruda's message became more political as he attempted to achieve justice and dignity for the deprived. It is this period that we shall analyze in Part I of the present study.

Neruda won the Nobel Prize in 1971 and was cited by the Swedish Academy for "a poetry that with the action of an elemental force brings alive a continent's destiny and dreams." Any critical discussion of his literary contribution would be incomplete if it did not mention his life and work after 1950, and this period will be covered in Part II, somewhat more briefly.

I

A NEW CONCEPTION OF ART

In the works of Pablo Neruda, the first break with his
earlier poetry occurred when he published the last three sections of Tercera residencia, written between 1934 and 1943,
in which he takes a new stand as a poet committed to social
justice and drastically changes his conception of art. "Reunión bajo las nuevas banderas" is perhaps the most important poem in the collection because it introduces new social
and political themes in his poetry. It foreshadows the remaining two sections of Tercera residencia and the Canto
general and, as such, very much deserves the extensive critical attention it has received.[1] But before examining it in
detail, we should take note of some of the ways in which the
poetry of this period differs from that of the initial period.

Neruda's earlier poems deal with the formation of the
individual in a fundamental, psychological sense. Although
the poems of Tercera residencia recapitulate much of this
material, they emphasize not the struggle for mere existence,
but rather the struggle for a significant existence. Having
emerged as an organism alive in the world, the poet must
learn to live harmoniously with other human beings; he must
learn to transcend the apparent paradox of his dual (physical
and spiritual) nature, and find his relation to reality as a
reunified being and not as an alienated one.

Neruda realizes that he has been imprisoned in the
chaotic world of the two Residencias, a vast area beset by
inhospitability and impossible to incorporate into his own existence. He has not been able to see order in life's movement toward death, and his attempt to communicate has
failed. Neruda rejects this world of isolation and, with it,
his previous poetry:

Contemplating them now, I consider the poems of

18

Residencia en la tierra harmful.   These poems
must not be read by the youth in our countries.
These are poems impregnated with a brutal pessimism and anguish.   They do not spell out existence
but death.

Contemplándolos ahora, considero dañinos los poemas de Residencia en la tierra.   Estos poemas no
deben ser leídos por la juventud de nuestros países.
Son poemas que están empapados de un pesimismo
y angustia atroces.   No ayudan a vivir, ayudan a
morir. [2]

If his poems can only convey anguish and pessimism, then he
must repudiate them. [3]

    The poet who until the Spanish Civil War had not taken
a political stand, appears in the last three sections of Tercera residencia as a man moved by the plight of men, ready to
take sides and to give a new orientation to his art.

    He now proclaims that art is useless unless it can im-
prove the human condition or unless it can save mankind.   He
accepts the poetic tradition established by Góngora and Ca-
möens, Quevedo and Alighieri, but confesses that

        from them also I saw humanity break through mor-
        tal wounds, and they showed me with their struggle
        and their constructive work that culture cannot af-
        ford to be a closed heritage, nor an empty palace
        decoration.

        también de ellos he visto respirar la humanidad por
        heridas mortales, y ellos me han indicado con sus
        luchas y construcciones que la cultura no puede ser
        patrimonio cerrado, ni decoración vacía de palacio. [4]

    As a poet who has become committed to the cause of
brotherhood, Neruda willingly puts his art at the service of
social realism.   He adopts Mayakovsky's tenet that a writer
should be interested in truth, and considers decadent those
who are mainly concerned with ornamentation and style.   For
Neruda truth corresponds to reality.   But truth is not static.
It is a cocreation of self and object, an "I" and "Thou" relationship, a fusion of the artist with his art.   This union
leads to action, because truth is not self-contained bliss.   If
literature aims at ornamentation only, it does not reflect truth

and is being used to falsify reality. A writer should not di-
verge from truth. He should simply try to reach the people
and bring them a message of hope.

Confronted with the question of poetic creation for only
a minority and poetic creation for the common people, Neruda
opts for the latter:

> the people love the simple word, they seek it as
> they would a flag preparing for the fight, in order
> to comfort their wretchedness, the simple word can
> also come from us to seek the people.

> el pueblo ama la palabra, la busca como bandera
> de lucha, como consuelos de sus dolores, la pala-
> bra puede también salir de nosotros para buscar al
> pueblo. [5]

He then remembers what Antonio Machado had replied when
asked the same thing:

> 'What more could I ask for than to write for the
> people, only Shakespeare and Cervantes have been
> able to do this until now. '

> '¡Qué más quisiera yo que escribir para el pueblo,
> sólo Shakespeare y Cervantes han podido hacerlo
> hasta ahora! '[6]

Neruda is aware that he can fail, but he can no longer write
a poetry that is only concerned with his interior state:

> My poetry's bitter hours had to end. The melan-
> cholic subjectivism of my Veinte poemas de amor
> and the painful sufferings of Residencia en la tierra
> were reaching their limit. ... As an activist poet
> I fought against my own conceit. As a consequence,
> the debate between the real and the subjective was
> decided within my own self.

> Las horas amargas de me poesía debían terminar.
> El sujetivismo melancólico de mi Veinte poemas de
> amor o el patetismo doloroso de Residencia en la
> tierra tocaban a su fin. ... Como poeta activo com-
> batí mi propio ensimismamiento. Por eso el de-
> bate entre lo real y lo sujetivo se decidió dentro de
> mi propio ser. [7]

With a new conception of art, and a new image of himself as a poet dedicated to truth, it is understandable that the previous relationship Neruda has established with a world in a state of disintegration now appears improper and undesirable.

"Reunión bajo las nuevas banderas" points to a poetic conversion, a marked change in the works of Pablo Neruda. What has changed basically is his mental attitude or, as a critic puts it, "el temple de ánimo."[8] This conversion could be defined as the step from an hermetic individualism to a commitment to socialism. In neither of these two instances is man missing from the scene. But we are now faced with a new concept of what existence really means, especially in the relationship man-world. The "I-Thou" relationship becomes an essential bond between the poet and other human beings. As Neruda sees it, man needs other men to construct a better world. Each skill must be utilized towards that end.

In lyrical poetry the mental attitude corresponds to an image the poet has of himself and of the world, to a way of making us know his interior state--not as something arrived at through abstract meditation or determined by the subconscious, but as something experienced with full awareness during some phase of his life.

Prior to "Reunion bajo las nuevas banderas," Neruda had perceived a reality which was distorted and which represented a rejection of society and of rationality. The first two stanzas of the poem clearly reveal this. As the poet changes his "temple de ánimo," he shows that he now holds a privileged position. He is no longer contained in the dark chambers of his own interior state. He has stepped in the forefront of human consciousness, mainly because he has discovered the true meaning of his art. He is now convinced that if he can control the tools of language, he can write a poetry of prophecy and give to the rest of mankind the insight necessary to change one's life, as he changed his, so that it will be more in accord with reality than with a misrepresentation of it. His earlier poetry stood for misrepresentation. His new will bring hope to man.

Neruda begins "Reunión bajo las nuevas banderas" by asking a rhetorical question which evokes the obscurity of his previous poetry:

Who has lied?   The broken stem of the lily,
unsoundable, incomprehensible, all full of
wounds and obscure splendor!   Everything;
the norm fragmented into waves, the inexact
barrow of amber, the sour drops of the
tassel of corn!   I forged my existence in
this, I listened to the grievous salt: at
night I went to plant my roots: I discovered
the bitter earth: everything became for me
darkness or lightning: a secret wax
filled my head and scattered ashes in
my tracks.

¿Quién ha mentido?   El pie de la azucena
roto, insondable, oscurecido, todo lleno
de herida y resplandor oscuro!   Todo,
la norma de ola en ola en ola, el impre-
ciso túmulo del ámbar y las ásperas
gotas de la espiga!   Fundé mi pecho en esto,
escuché toda la sal funesta: de noche fui
a plantar mis raíces: averigüé lo amargo
de la tierra: todo fue para mí noche o
relámpago: cera secreta cupo en mi cabeza
y derramó cenizas en mis huellas [OC 250].

The answer to the question, however, is not as important as
the realization that the poetic world of the first two Residencias, full of images representing the bitterness on earth, is
a perversion of truth.   It does not matter whether it was the
world which fraudulently presented itself in a deformed
fashion ("El pie de la azucena roto, insondable, oscurecido,
todo lleno de herida y resplandor oscuro!"), or whether
it was the poet's fault for perceiving such a distorted reality
and for forging his existence in it ("Fundé mi pecho en esto").
More essential to the poet and to his art is the fact that his
mental attitude has changed.   Neruda feels the need to de-
nounce his previous state as false, since the reality it has
reflected--symbolized by the wilted flower--is painful and de-
ceptive.   Such a reality can only bring him into a direct contact with death--the same death which hovered over Residencia en la tierra II, which became the great isolator, which
pervaded his existence and accompanied him everywhere.

The rhetorical interrogation of the second stanza brings
back the theme of death so typical of Residencia en la tierra
II:

And for whom did I seek this cold pulse
if not for a death?
And what instrument did I lose in the
forsaken darkness, where no one hears me?
No,
   It was about time; flee
shadows of blood,
chills of star, retrieve your step from
   human steps
and keep the black shadow at a distance from
   my feet!

¿Y pare quién busqué este pulso frío
sino para una muerte?
¿Y qué instrumento perdí en las tinieblas
desamparadas, donde nadie me oye?
No,
   ya era tiempo, huid
sombras de sangre,
hielos de estrella, retroceded al paso de
   los pasos humanos
y alejad de mis pies la negra sombra! [OC 250].

Mario Rodríguez Fernández points out that it is not death but "a death" described here by Neruda. It is a death born out of solitary existence that eschews the social. It is not death in general, but a death that represents the poet's own. It is a specific way of dying, the result of a specific way of living. [9]

This way of life, in complete alienation from the rest of the world, emphasizes the poet's isolation and loss of orientation. He is like the sea captain without a compass, or without the guidance of a lighthouse. Darkness and the unknown do not offer him any refuge, and any possibility of communication is denied him (just as it had happened in the Veinte poemas de amor, where any spiritual relationship with the beloved was thwarted).

Neruda feels that he has spent too much time on the subject of death and wants to turn to an acceptance of life. If his early poetry has dealt with nothing more than anguish, it must be rejected by the poet. Up to this point, Neruda's existence has thrived on dark shadows. He must run away from the "sombras de sangre," and reject the dark side of his life and the conditions that brought this state of being, in order to establish a firm spiritual bond with men. "No, ya era tiempo, huid ... " [OC 250].

The world of the first two Residencias has held the poet prisoner because of its absurdity and impenetrability. In "Unidad" Neruda feels oppressed by facticity: stones, wood, wool, mineral.   "Me rodea una misma cosa" he tells us.   And then, to make his state of imprisonment even more desperate, he adds: "Las cosas se unen en torno a mí como paredes."   Now the poet is willing to give up materiality for spirituality, disillusionment for faith, anguish for enthusiasm, solitude for solidarity, and the obscurity of his subconscious for full consciousness and clarity.

It is evident that to achieve this transformation the poet needs a new set of images and a new language, and "Reunión bajo las nuevas banderas" represents a transition to this new language:

> As other men, I have the same wounded hand,
> I sustain the same red goblet,
> I share the same infuriating fear:
> > on a day
> palpitating with human dreams,
> a wild cereal has entered
> my devouring night
> so that I can join my steps of wolf
> to human steps.

> Yo de los hombres tengo la misma mano herida
> yo sostengo la misma copa roja
> he igual asombro enfurecido:
> > un día
> palpitante de sueños
> humanos, un salvaje
> cereal ha llegado
> a mi devoradora noche
> para que junte mis pasos de lobo
> a los pasos de hombre [OC 250-1].

The poet is a man who has given up his solitary place in the world and has joined in communion with other men.   The images "Mano herida/asombro enfurecido" suggest that this new life is not easy, but because it is shared with other men-- "sostengo la misma copa roja"--it offers hope for survival.

In the first two stanzas of the poem, Neruda uses the past tense to bring back the earlier poetry of affliction and anguish, and to point to his old mental attitude.   In the third stanza he uses the present tense as an indication that he has a new "temple de ánimo." He will be in solidarity with humanity whether it be in pain, hope or anger. The loneliness of the devouring night will subside as soon as he shares in the existence of the human race.

The ties with humanity permit the poet to take another look at himself. His main feat is to overcome darkness: it is the long-hoped-for and expected triumph of consciousness over the unconscious (day and light are synonymous for consciousness, night and dark for the unconscious). Neruda, searching for true existence, will no longer indulge in self pity, nor will he weaken and lament his state. He has no more room for sentimentality and will now sing of the most sacred values of man: free will, constructive work, and most of all fraternity.

> And thus, reunited,
> strictly within my self, I do not seek asylum
> in hollow tears: I show off
> the hive bee stock, radiant bread
> for the son of man: within the mystery,
> the azure gets ready to contemplate
> a distant wheat of blood.

> Y así, reunido
> duramente central, no busco asilo
> en los huecos del llanto: muestro
> la cepa de la abeja, pan radiante
> para el hijo del hombre: en el misterio
> el azul se prepara para mirar
> un trigo lejano de la sangre [OC 251].

Man needs bread. But it must be worked for and man must imitate the productive insects, such as the bee, to provide for human needs. The imagery of bread and blood, the same components used in the Catholic sacrament of the Eucharist, may have been used here to represent the same idea of "communion." This is not a communion, however, between God and man, but between man and man.

In the next series of interrogations, following the pattern of the other questions in the poem, Neruda recalls some typical imagery and symbols of his earlier poetry, and then rejects them:

> Where is your place in a rose?
> Where is your starred eyelid?

Did you forget those sweaty
crazy fingers which try to reach the sand?

¿Dónde está tu sitio en la rosa?
¿En dónde está tu párpado de estrellas?
¿Olvidaste esos dedos de sudor que enloquecen
para alcanzar la arena? [OC 251].

He inquires what has happened to his former eroticism, so
frequently expressed with the image of a rose (for example,
in the first poem of Veinte poemas de amor, Neruda asso-
ciates this flower with the pubes-- "¡Ah las rosas del pubis!").
He questions his cold poetic attitude, often expressed in Residencia en la tierra, and recalls the frenetic movement of his
fingers which seem to be out of control for a useless activity.

The answer to all these questions is the same: a repudiation of what he has written in the past.   The last image
of fingers that sweat is symbolic of Neruda's struggle as a
poet who uses introspection.   The hour has come to get rid
of his "ensimismamiento," to get rid of the anguish in him
which has falsified reality and has made him shirk his responsibilities as a man.   He needs peace to devote himself
to the cause of humanity and make every one of his activities,
especially that of being a poet, mean something:

Peace to you, somber sun,
Peace to you, blind forehead ...

Paz para ti, sol sombrío,
paz para ti, frente ciega ... [OC 251].

Neruda feels that he must sing of what awaits him on the
road, in the stones, in the suffering of mankind:

There is a burning place for you on the road,
there are stones devoid of mystery which look
    at you,
there are silences of prison and a crazy star,
naked, coarse, contemplating hell.

Hay un quemante sitio para tí en los caminos,
hay piedras sin misterio que te miran,
hay silencios de cárcel con una estrella loca,
desnuda, desbocada, contemplando el infierno
    [OC 251].

What confronts him is the continuous agitation of life, and
the silent suffering of those who are maltreated by others.
The road ahead is not smooth, and a burning path awaits the
poet. The surroundin reality has changed: the stones do
not any longer contain he mystery of many generations.
They are stones withou secrecy watching the poet as he pro-
gresses on his journey. Neruda has found himself and is
sure of the road ahead. He is fully conscious of the task
that awaits him. In the face of despair and suffering, he is
indissolubly bound to other men:

>Together, confronted with sobbing!
>   It is the solemn hour
>of earth and perfume, look at this visage
>recently emerged from the terrible salt,
>look at this bitter mouth which smiles,
>look at this new heart which salutes you
>with its uncontainable flower, determined
>   and golden.

>Juntos, fr nte al sollozo!
>   Es la hora
>alta de t.erra y perfume, mirad este rostro
>recién salido de la sal terrible,
>mirad esta boca amarga que sonríe,
>mirad este nuevo corazón que os saluda
>con su flor desbordante, determinada y áurea
>   [OC 251].

As the title implies, "Reunión bajo las nuevas banderas" is indeed a poem of renewal. Drawing upon his previous imagery--"sal terrible, " "boca amarga"--Neruda paves
the way for the great poems of the Canto general. The disintegrating state of his soul in a disintegrating world has
been replaced by an attitude reflecting optimism. He has
abandoned the image of salt, often used in his earlier poetry
to stand for corruption. There has been a change of heart
in Neruda, and his existence has acquired a new meaning,
exemplified by the last two lines of the poem. The same attitude of optimism will be reflected in his social and political
poetry.

Solidarity has led Neruda to the discovery of the world
of the working man and of collective efforts. The poet shows
his face, that of a true believer, so that all can see him
("Mirad este nuevo corazón que os saluda"). It is no mere
accident that when the Spanish Civil War breaks, Neruda will

take up his verse as if it were a weapon. He is no longer the solitary poet apart from the rest. He is a man united to other men, to the fighting people of Spain, and his contribution to the cause will be <u>España en el corazón</u>.

The third section of <u>Tercera residencia</u> establishes the crucial imagery for "Reunión bajo las nuevas banderas, " and to a certain extent for the poetry that follows, and is also a demonstration of Neruda's new conception of art. One could say that "Reunión bajo las nuevas banderas" represents the "Arte poética" of this social and political phase of his writings, and the model that he will follow during the next two decades.

The section is perfectly structured. It opens with the image of a flower cut at the base, which suggests that the flower is dying, and ends with the image of a flower blossoming. Both images reflect Neruda's earlier and later poetry, respectively, his old "temple de ánimo" and his new attitude toward the world. The interrogations in the poem evoke the previous poetry, from which he slowly breaks away.

In the first stanza of the poem, Neruda objectifies his old mental state and establishes a distance between his poetic past and the present. The second stanza begins with two rhetorical questions used by the poet, as we have seen, to recall and reject his anguished past. In the third stanza, Neruda comes into contact with a world that has order, is familiar and provides shelter. The poem ends with a note of optimism. Neruda proclaims his newly found salvation. He has encountered truth, and the saving grace has descended upon his being. The progression from a negative attitude with respect to the world to a positive one can easily be followed from the first to the last stanza of this poem.

The evolution of a writer--like the evolution of poetry itself--is based on innovations. But at the same time, it leaves much unchanged. Although Neruda's poetry undergoes a profound change with "Reunión bajo las nuevas banderas, " this does not mean, as some critics and Neruda himself would want us to believe, that his poetry has totally rejected the previous phases.

The old Neruda can be detected in the new poems, even if the tone has changed; the same style, even if altered; the same powerful language, even if it is cried out violently at times. The imagery is still original (as it has been since

the Veinte poemas de amor).   But before, the image-symbols
were literally poured out one after another, leaving very little
understanding as to their meaning.   For example, "El reloj
caído en el mar," from Residencia en la tierra II, is a much
more difficult poem to interpret than "Reunión bajo las nuevas
banderas."   The poet was using a hermetic poetry which was
obscure for the most part.   Now Neruda will no longer remain completely hidden by his imagery, and, instead of using
the language of introspection, he will use the language of proclamation in declaring his new mission as a poet.[10]

   Residencia en la tierra I and II, and the first two sections of Tercera residencia, offer no salvation to the poet who
is lost in the chaos of existence.   The "temple de ánimo" expressed in this poetry of destruction and death is a very dra-
matic one, singled out by unresolved tensions and by anguish.
The poet moves in an inhospitable world, feels insecure and
lonely, like a shipwrecked person without any land beneath
him.   Fernando Alegría, analyzing the poetry of this period,
has maintained that in dealing with monumental chaos and
death Neruda has expressed as no other poet before him the
metaphysical anguish of the Hispanic American man.[11]

   "Reunión bajo las nuevas banderas" brings the newly
found grace which had been denied to the "hombre residen-
ciario."   We are confronted with a new poet, who proclaims
a new function for his lyric poetry, where the social stands
above the personal, and where altruism replaces egotism.
Neruda rejects his earlier poetry and looks at reality from
a different perspective.

   Section III of Tercera residencia marks the precise
moment of a poetic conversion in Neruda.   The political and
social themes are introduced and will become the most important consideration of the poet for the next two decades or
more.   The remaining two sections of Tercera residencia,
and the Canto general are good examples of Neruda's social
poetry with political overtones.

II

ESPAÑA EN EL CORAZÓN

España en el corazón; himno a las glorias del pueblo
en guerra introduces in the poetry of Pablo Neruda the political themes prefigured in "Reunión bajo las nuevas banderas." Until the publication of this book in 1937, many elements of Neruda's poetry were related to the theme of death
or to an expression of solitude in terms of an alien environment, infinite in extent and devoid of reason. What characterizes the new poetry instead is a feeling of hope and confi-
dence in the future of mankind. Neruda will now write inspired by the heroism of the Spanish people at war.

In España en el corazón Neruda utilizes different colors to present a portrait of the Spain of the Civil War:
white represents the hope of the Republican fighters; black,
the defeat of the Fascists. The book describes death as the
seed of a new and better life. Each drop of blood signifies
hope for the future. Time shall bring victory as well as the
eventual defeat of Francisco Franco and his forces.

When the Spanish Civil War began in the summer of
1936, Neruda had already lived in Spain as Chilean consul for
two years. He had arrived in Barcelona on May 5, 1934.
Shortly after he rented a house in Madrid with the help of
Rafael Alberti. He also kept in contact with other Spanish
poets and intellectuals--García Lorca, Miguel Hernández,
Manuel Altolaguirre, and Arturo Serrano Plaja among them.

Neruda was in the Spanish capital when the loyalist
forces, led by Franco, rebelled against the Republican Government which had been in power since 1931. The poet witnessed the clash and recorded his impressions of Madrid:

> And one morning the bonfires
> emerged from the earth

30

swallowing beings,
and since then fire,
dust since then,
and since then blood.

Y una mañana las hogueras
salían de la tierra
devorando seres,
y desde entonces fuego,
pólvora desde entonces,
y desde entonces sangre [OC 255-6].

As Chilean consul, Neruda theoretically should have
remained neutral. But the death of García Lorca, and the
political activism of Rafael Alberti and Manuel Altolaguirre,
made him join an increasing number of Spanish and Hispanic
American intellectuals who identified themselves with the
plight of the Republic.

Three months after the outbreak of violence in Spain,
Neruda left his consular post in Madrid and went to Paris to
stir interest for the Republican cause. On November 7, 1936,
with Nancy Cunard he published an article entitled "Los poetas del mundo defienden al pueblo español." In February of
the following year, Neruda gave a lecture on Federico García Lorca (which is included in the Obras completas). While
in Paris, he also met the Peruvian poet César Vallejo. The
two organized a charitable society, known as the "Grupo His-
pano-americano de Ayuda a España," to help the Spanish Republican Government in power. In July, 1937, Neruda par-
ticipated in the Congress of American Nations, and a few
weeks later he returned to Spain to attend the Second Congress
of Writers held in Valencia, the capital of the Spanish Republic. He also returned for a few days to Madrid, where he
witnessed the Falangist bombardment of the city. Neruda
again left Spain for France, to request French participation
in the Civil War. He lectured in universities, held meetings
with Spanish exiles and other interested parties, distributed
propaganda pamphlets, and defended the Spanish Republicans.
Because of such overt participation, Neruda lost his diplomatic post and was recalled by the Chilean government. [1]

On the ship returning to Chile, Neruda finished España en el corazón. This collection of poems on the Civil
War was published in Santiago on November 13, 1937, as
Section IV of Tercera residencia. A year later, on November 7, España en el corazón appeared in Spain under sepa-

rate cover, in book format.   The first 500 copies were edited by Manuel Altolaguirre and published on the battlefield. The soldiers themselves made paper and did the printing. Altolaguirre writes in the "Prologue" of this historical edition:

> The great poet Pablo Neruda (the most profound voice of America since Rubén Darío, as García Lorca said), lived with us the first months of the war.   Later, at sea, as from an island in exile, he wrote the poems of this book.   The Commissariat of the Eastern Army reprinted it in Spain. Those who made the paper, produced the text, and operated the machines are soldiers of the Republic. Let the poet friend receive this news as a dedicatory.

> El gran poeta Pablo Neruda (la voz más profunda de América desde Rubén Darío, como dijo García Lorca), convivió con nosotros los primeros meses de la guerra.   Luego, en el mar, como desde un destierro, escribió los poemas de este libro.   El Comisariado del Ejército del Este lo reimprime en España.   Son soldados de la República quienes fabricaron el papel, compusieron el texto y movieron las máquinas.   Reciba el poeta amigo esta noticia como una dedicatoria. [2]

From this date on, the poet Neruda and the activist committed to social justice are one and the same.   However, his poetry did not deal only with social or political themes, although these are predominant in the period 1936-1950, and he did not consider himself either a Communist or a Socialist. On his arrival in Santiago, in 1937, Neruda told the press:

> I am not a Communist.   Nor a Socialist.   Nor anything.   I am, simply, a writer.   A free writer who loves liberty with simplicity.   I love the people.   I belong to them because I come from them.   That is why I am anti-fascist.   My loyalty to the people does not smack of orthodoxy nor of sentiment.

> Yo no soy comunista.   Ni socialista.   Ni nada. Soy, simplemente, escritor.   Escritor libre, que ama la libertad con sencillez.   Amo al pueblo. Pertenezco a él porque de él vengo.   Por ello soy antifascista.   Mi adhesión al pueblo no peca de ortodoxia ni de sentimiento. [3]

His mission as a poet was clear to him: to fight
fascism and to become the spokesman of the suffering masses
in Spain and in Latin America.   It was not until 1945 that Neruda formally rejected his apolitical stand and became a militant member of the Communist Party.

The major theme of España en el corazón is political:
Neruda takes sides with the people of Spain and he condemns
the fascists for wanting to usurp power from a democratically
elected government.   It is because of its political content that
the book has been judged by some critics--Alfredo Cardona
Peña among them--to be one of Neruda's best.   Others, including Raúl Silva Castro, have rejected it because according
to their artistic standards, the merit of a literary creation
is lessened by the expression of a political ideology.   Both
views are equally invalid in their absolute sense: there are
poems in the book which are merely propagandistic and prosaic, such as "España pobre por culpa de los ricos"; others
have definite artistic merit, such as "Cómo era España," or
"Canto sobre las ruinas," and will be analyzed later.

Bernard Gicovate disagrees with Silva Castro, who di-
vides Neruda's poetry into categories of good and bad, quali-
fying as good his apolitical poems and as bad his political
ones:

> On the contrary, if we find in Neruda's poetry aesthe-
> tic values indissolubly united to his political thought,
> we will have to accept the possibility of the existence
> of a partisan poetry which at the same time can in-
> struct because of its expressive worth.... [I]t can
> very well be that some poems in our time acquire
> value through the same force of conviction that
> helped produce them.

> Por el contrario, si se encuentran en la poesía de
> Neruda valores estéticos indisolublemente unidos a
> su pensamiento político, tendremos que aceptar la
> posibilidad de la existencia de poesía partidaria que
> al mismo tiempo pueda imponerse por su valor ex-
> presivo.... [P]uede muy bien ser posible que algu-
> nos poemas de nuestro tiempo adquieran valor por la
> misma fuerza de las convicciones que los han produ-
> cido. [4]

As Rubén Darío so well demonstrated in his later works, there
is room in poetry for the social and the political.

The Spanish Civil War inspired many works of art, especially in poetry. Not only Neruda, but other Spanish-speaking poets devoted much of their attention to the event. In 1936 Rafael Alberti published the ballad, Romance de la guerra española. A year later Nicolás Guillén wrote a poem divided into five parts, entitled España, poema en cuatro angustias y una esperanza. César Vallejo's contribution in 1938 was España, aparta de mí este cáliz. Other famous Europeans wrote on the subject too: in France, Paul Eluard and Louis Aragon; in England, Stephen Spender, Winston Hugh Andrew and Cecil Day Lewis; and, in Germany, Bertold Brecht.

Neruda, able to obtain a firsthand account of the war as a resident of Madrid, reexamined his task as a poet and accepted a change of orientation in his lyrical poetry. Rather than being a poet of death, of melancholy and of defeat, he became a poet in support of the deprived people.

As a poet very much preoccupied with his artistic creation and with his audience, Neruda felt compelled to justify his change of attitude. In a brief note inserted before the poem "Las furias y las penas," in March 1939, he explained what had caused the change:

> This poem was written in 1934 (The Furies and
> Sorrows). How many things have happened since
> then. Spain, where I wrote it, is a belt of ruins.
> Alas! if we could appease the ire of the world with
> only one drop of poetry or love; this, however, only
> the fighting and the heart can resolve. The world
> has changed and my poetry has changed. One drop
> of blood fallen on these lines goes on living upon
> them, indelible as love.

> En 1934 fue escrito este poema (Las furias y las
> penas). Cuántas cosas han sobrevenido desde en-
> tonces! España, donde lo escribí, es una cintura
> de ruinas. Ay! si con una sola gota de poesía o
> de amor pudiéramos aplacar la ira del mundo, pe-
> ro eso sólo lo pueden la lucha y el corazón resuel-
> to. El mundo ha cambiado y mi poesía ha cambiado.
> Una gota de sangre caída en estas líneas quedará
> viviendo sobre ellas, indeleble como el amor [OC
> 244].

Neruda's experience in Spain during the Civil War altered the entire course of his poetry. As a man witnessing

the horrors of the first three months of the conflict, he con-
cluded that his old poetic world, afflicted by solitude and anguish, had to be replaced by a new one based on hope and
faith. His preoccupation with his personal existence, and his
metaphysical poetry so characteristic of Residencia en la
tierra I and II, were abandoned for a preoccupation with all
men's suffering, and a poetry oriented toward social realism.

In "Explico algunas cosas," Neruda once again makes
use of rhetorical questions which imply the rejection of his
previous poetry:

> You will ask: And where are the lilacs?
> And the metaphysics petalled with poppies?
> And the rain repeatedly spattering
> its words, filling them
> with holes and birds?
> . . .
> You will ask why his poetry
> doesn't speak of dreams and leaves,
> and of the great volcanoes of his birthplace?
>
> Come see the blood in the streets,
> Come see
> the blood in the streets,
> Come see the blood
> in the streets!
>
> Preguntaréis: Y dónde están las lilas?
> y la metafísica cubierta de amapolas?
> y la lluvia que a menudo golpeaba
> sus palabras llenándolas
> de agujeros y pájaros?
> . . .
> Preguntaréis por qué su poesía
> no nos habla del sueño, de las hojas,
> de los grandes volcanes de su país natal?
>
> Venid a ver la sangre por las calles,
> venid a ver
> la sangre por las calles,
> venid a ver la sangre
> por las calles! [OC 254-6]

In that same year, Neruda rejected a poetry far removed
from the real world. [5] In Canto general, however, he once
again sang of the torrential rains of the south and the majes-

tic volcanoes that hover over the long and narrow Andean
country of Chile. Neruda felt it inappropriate, in the midst
of a bloody civil strife, to write lyric poetry exalting the
beauty of nature. And he made the change. Seeing blood in
the streets caused Neruda to make the transition from a poetry that expresses the tormented interior state of one man to
a poetry that reflects the suffering of many.

España en el corazón begins with an invocation. The
muse is Spain and the poet's desire is to write an explosive
chant that will expose conditions in the country after the beginning of the three-year war. The bombardment of the
Spanish capital comes next, and the poet's anger reaches its
culminating point in "Maldición," in which he portrays Spain
as being murdered by bandits and Moors, the only people that
would fight on the side of the Fascists, and condemns those
responsible for the unjust war. Spain is poor because of the
rich, and the wealth has been accumulated in the hands of the
corrupt monarchy, the church and the generals. These are
the ones who have betrayed their fatherland and have reduced
Madrid to a heap of ruins.

In that month of July, 1936, Neruda remembers that
Madrid was a happy city:

> I lived in a suburb
> of Madrid, with bells
> and clocks and trees.
> From there you could see
> the dry face of Castille
> like an ocean of leather.
>   My house was called
> the house of flowers, because everywhere
> geraniums grew: it was a
> beautiful house
> with dogs and children.
>   Remember, Raul?
> remember, Rafael?
>   Federico, do you remember
> from under the earth,
> do you remember my house with balconies where
> the light of June drowned flowers in your mouth
> ...
> And one morning all was burning...

> Yo vivía en un barrio
> de Madrid, con campanas,

con relojes, con árboles.
Desde allí se veía
el rostro seco de Castilla
como un océano de cuero.
                    Mi casa era llamada
la casa de las flores, porque por todas partes
estallaban geranios: era
una bella casa
con perro y chiquillos.
                    Raúl, te acuerdas?
Te acuerdas, Rafael?
                    Federico, te acuerdas
debajo de la tierra,
te acuerdas de mi casa con balcones en donde
la luz de junio ahogaba flores en tu boca?
...
Y una mañana todo estaba ardiendo ... [OC 255].

But suddenly the first shot is fired.   The happy appearance of
the city is smeared in blood.   Madrid is wounded and tries to
defend herself, while the generals carefully plan her destruction.

Neruda vehemently denounces their actions and sees in
the burning of the city a symbol of hope for the Republicans
and of defeat for the Fascists.   He accuses the generals and
warns them of the fate that awaits traitors:

Generals
traitors:
look at my house void of life,
look at Spain, broken:
but from every dying house burning metal flows
instead of flowers,
from every hollow of Spain
Spain emerges,
and from every dead child a rifle with eyes,
and from every crime bullets
that will one day
find you--in the heart.

Generales
traidores:
mirad mi casa muerta,
mirad España rota:
pero de cada casa muerta sale metal ardiendo
en vez de flores,

> pero de cada hueco de España
> sale España,
> pero de cada niño muerto sale un fusil con ojos,
> pero de cada crimen nacen balas
> que os hallarán un día el sitio
> del corazón [OC 256]

In the poem that follows, "Canto a las madres de los mili-
cianos muertos," Neruda abandons his passionate tone of
anger to console the mothers of the young Republicans who
lost their lives in battle. He assures them that their sons'
sacrifices were not in vain. Their sons are smiling from
the ground on which they died because they understand that
their deaths were necessary for a greater good, to bring
about the ultimate triumph of the Republic. In a subdued
tone, Neruda describes pre-war Spain in "Cómo era España."
For its musicality, the poem is considered one of the high-
lights of the book and has been compared to Antonio Machado's
"Campos de Castilla."[6]

"Cómo era España" is a poem divided into 18 stanzas.
In the last 14, Neruda names 124 Spanish towns, arranging
them in quartets. The resonance of the names produces the
effect of a psalmody. The first four stanzas comprise a unit
by themselves and could very well be a poem independent of
what follows. Spain is pure among the nations of the world
and the poet expresses his deep love for her.

The next two poems, "Llegada a Madrid de la Brigada
Internacional," and the "Batalla del río Jarama," once again
depict the Spanish nation torn by war. In the first, using a
metrical pattern very similar to that of "Nocturno III," by
José Asunción Silva, Neruda sees hope in the arrival of the
International Brigade:

> On the morning of a very cold month,
> an agonizing month, soiled by mud and by smoke,
> a month without knees, a sorrowful month of
>   siege and misfortune,
> when across the windowpanes of my house the
>   African jackals were heard
> howling with their rifles and their teeth full
>   of blood,
> then,
> when we had no more hope than a dream of gunpowder,
> when we thought
> that the whole world was only full of devouring
>   monsters and furies,

then, breaking the frost of this frozen month
        in Madrid
amidst the fog of dawn
I saw with these very eyes, with this heart
        that sees,
the arrival of the celebrated ones,
the towering soldiers
of the slender and hard and seasoned and
        ardent brigade of stone.

Una mañana de un mes frío,
de un mes agonizante, manchado por el lodo y por
        el humo,
un mes sin rodillas, un triste mes de sitio y
        desventura,
cuando a través de los cristales mojados de mi
        casa se oían los chacales africanos
aullar con los rifles y los dientes llenos de
        sangre, entonces,
cuando no teníamos más esperanza que un sueño
        de pólvora, cuando ya creíamos
que el mondo estaba lleno solo de monstruos
        devoradores y de furias,
entonces, quebrando la escarcha del mes de frío
        de Madrid, en la niebla
del alba
he visto con estos ojos que tengo, con este
        corazón que mira,
he visto llegar a los claros, a los diminadores
        combatientes
de la delgada y dura y madura y ardiente
        brigada de piedra [OC 260-1].

It is evident that Neruda falls short of achieving the rhythm
and musicality of Asunción Silva's poem, and yet he achieves
a powerful emotional effect.

The "Batalla del río Jarama" is one of the best-struc-
tured poems in the book. Neruda returns to the measured
stanza and to his favorite meter, the hendecasyllable. The
poem has nine stanzas of four verses each. The first three
verses have 11 syllables, the last one has seven.

In the poem Neruda praises the heroic resistance of
the river which did not succumb to the wave of barbarians--
symbolic of the Fascists--who invaded its shores:

Between the land and the drowned platinum
of olive groves and dead Spaniards,
Jarama, pure dagger, you have resisted
the wave of the cruel barbarians.

Entre la tierra y el platino ahogado
de olivares y muertos españoles,
Jarama, puñal puro, ha resistido
        la ola de los crueles [OC 262].

The people from nearby towns are also by the riverside to defend it:

The harsh flour of your people was
spiked with metals and bones,
formidable and wheat-bearing like the noble
land they were defending.

La áspera harina de tu pueblo estaba
toda erizada de metal y huesos,
formidable y trigal como la noble
        tierra que defendían [OC 263].

And Neruda concludes the poem with a personification of the river and its surroundings, which is at once simple and suggestive:

Your grievous sky remains there,
your peace like stone, your stellar stream,
and the eternal eyes of your people
keep vigilance on your shores.

Allí quedan tu cielo doloroso,
tu paz de piedra, tu estelar corriente,
y los eternos ojos de tu pueblo
        vigilan tus orillas [OC 263].

In the next five poems of the book, Neruda returns to his accusatory tone: In "Almería" the poet gives to the clergy, the military and the businessmen a symbolic plate which contains the blood of those fighting for the defense of Spain; in "Tierras ofendidas," Neruda tells us that not even victory can restore the beauty that was once evident in the Spanish countryside; in the three poems that follow, he places generals Sanjurjo, Mola, and Franco in hell, for the crimes they have committed.

The best poem of the three is "Mola en los infiernos, " in which Neruda uses the tone so typical of Quevedo, Quintana, and other lyric poets who have denounced conditions in Spain. But Neruda comes closest to Quevedo for the subtle, ironic caricature of Mola:

> The thick and mulish Mola
> dragged forever from abyss to abyss,
> broken up by brimstone and horn
> as a shipwreck pitched from wave to wave,
> boiled in lime and ice and pretense,
> long awaited in hell,
> is on his way;
> infernal mulatto, this son of a jackass,
> stubborn greenhorn,
> flames up his tail and up his ass.

> Es arrastrado el turbio mulo Mola
> de precipicio en precipicio eterno
> y como va el naufragio de ola en ola,
> desbaratado por azufre y cuerno,
> cocido en cal y hielo y disimulo,
> de antemano esperado en el infierno,
> va el infernal mulato, el Mola mulo
> definitivamente turbio y tierno,
> con llamas en la cola y en el culo [OC 265].

"Canto sobre las ruinas" represents the best lyrical effort of Neruda in the entire book.   The lugubrious vision of some ruins--the place is not specified--moves the poet to lament the absurdity of war and the tragedy of destruction. All that has been laboriously constructed with human efforts has been wiped out by the armed conflict.

Using a chaotic enumeration of objects, typical of Residencia en la tierra I and II, Neruda intensifies the feeling of destruction.   This time, however, the disintegration of the familiar world is brought about not by an alien environment, incomprehensible and inhospitable, but by wicked men. Since the cause has been determined, Neruda feels that he, as a just man, can do something to help eradicate it.

In the last two stanzas of the poem, the contrast between peace and tranquility as opposed to devastation is emphasized by effective metaphors which make the tone of the poem elegiac.   Thus the times of prosperity and peace are represented by the image of doves with a white waist made of flour ("palomas con cintura de harina"), or by a fragrant young girl in love, the symbol of joyous life. The hour of extermination is objectified in disintegrating matter or in the image of the same young girl who no longer represents contentment:

> See how the guitar
> has rotted in the mouth of the fragrant
>   young girl:
> see how the words which used to build
>   so much
> now destroy: beyond the lime and the
>   dissolved marble
> look for a trace of tears, already covered
>   with moss

> Ved cómo se ha podrido
> la guitarra en la boca de la fragrante novia:
> ved cómo las palabras que tanto construyeron,
> ahora son exterminio: mirad sobre la cal y
>   entre el mármol deshecho
> la huella--ya con musgos--del sollozo [OC 268].

España en el corazón ends with the poem "Oda solar al ejército del pueblo," in which Neruda salutes the common workers, miners, railroaders, photographers, carpenters. The Spanish people are symbolized by a group of soldiers marching to ultimate triumph:

> ... onward, Spain,
> onward, bells of the people,
> onward, regions of apples,
> onward, cerealian banners,
> onward, experts of the fire,
> because in battle, in the wave, in the prairie,
> in the mountains, in the heavy twilight of
>   harsh aroma,
> you bear a source of permanence, a thread
> difficult to break.

> ... adelante, España,
> adelante, campanas populares,
> adelante, regiones de manzana,
> adelante, estandartes cereales,
> adelante, mayúsculos del fuego,
> porque en la lucha, en la ola, en la pradera,
> en la montaña, en el crepúsculo cargado de
>   acre aroma,

lleváis un nacimiento de parmanencia, un hilo
de difícil dureza [OC 274].

Viewed as a unit, España en el corazón, like other
books of poetry that have reflected social realism and have
made use of political themes, gives us a glimpse of a poetry
of uneven quality.   One must keep in mind, however, that
the political or social themes, in themselves, are not responsible for the artistic quality of the poems.   The quality of a
poem depends not on its themes but on the artistry of its
author.   The same theme can inspire a good poem as it can
a prosaic or propagandistic one.

Neruda's preoccupation during this period, to write
poetry that can be clearly understood by the common man,
can at times turn his material into prose.   An example of
this can be found in the first five lines of the poem "España
pobre por culpa de los ricos:"

> Cursed be those that one day
> didn't look, cursed be those damned blind ones
> who offered to their solemn land
> tears and not bread, cursed be
> those stained uniforms and the clergy ...

> Malditos los que un día
> no miraron, malditos ciegos malditos
> los que no adelantaron a la solemne patria
> el pan sino las lágrimas, malditos
> uniformes manchados y sotanas ... [OC 253].

And the same prosaic verse will be repeated by Neruda in
his diatribes against dictators in Hispanic America, in the
Canto general.

In spite of the prosaic verses cited above, España en
el corazón has many subtle and suggestive lines of poetry,
such as these:

> Taut and dry was Spain,
> a daily drum of dull sound,
> a prairie, an eagle eyrie, a silence
> scoured by brutal weather.

> Era España tirante y seca, diurno
> tambor de son opaco,
> llanura y nido de águilas, silencio
> de azotada intemperie [OC 258].

The book still contains the original imagery typical of
Neruda's earlier works, the enumeration of images and objects, which once again will be used in Canto general, as
well as an essential thematic unity. In España en el corazón the poet discovers that unity in the Spanish Civil War and
speaks of the sacrifices and fraternity he observed in those
who--like the men of the International Brigade--have risen in
defense of liberty.

A change of orientation in the works of a poet is not
new. Dante and Quevedo, and more recently Rubén Darío,
have all used social and political themes to express their dis-
enchantment with the prevailing situation in their countries
and in the world. Within their own poems both Darío and
Neruda acknowledge that a change in their poetry had taken
place. [7] In "De otoño," the Nicaraguan tells us:

> I know that there are those who say: why
>   doesn't he sing now
> with the madness of yesteryears?

> Yo sé que hay quienes dicen: ¿ Por qué
>   no canta ahora
> con aquella locura de antaño? [8]

And Neruda, in "Explico algunas cosas," repeats the same
rhetorical question:

> You will ask: And where are the lilacs?
> And the metaphysics petalled with poppies?

> Preguntaréis: Y dónde están las lilas?
> Y la metafísica cubierta de amapolas? [OC 254].

Moreover, those well-known hendecasyllables, prover-
bial in indicating the change that has occurred in the two
poets, have a similarity that extends far beyond their metrical pattern. In the first poem of Cantos de vida y esperanza
Darío writes:

> I am that one who yesterday was only singing
> the blue verse and the profane song,
> where in the evening there was a nightingale
> that was a lark in the morning light.

> Yo soy aquel que ayer no más decía
> el verso azul y la canción profana,

en cuya noche un ruiseñor había
que era alondra de luz por la mañana. [9]

In "Nuevo canto de amor a Stalingrado," using the same meter and the same rhyme, and as if paraphrasing the Nicaraguan, Neruda says:

> I wrote about time and about water
> I described bereavement and its murrey metal,
> I wrote about the sky and about apples,
> now I write about Stalingrad.

> Yo escribí sobre el tiempo y sobre el agua
> describí el luto y su metal morado,
> yo escribí sobre el cielo y la manzana,
> ahora escribo sobre Stalingrado [OC 277].

Section V of Tercera residencia, which immediately
follows España en el corazón, is the least interesting because of its subject matter.   It contains two poems: "Canto
a Stalingrado," and "Nuevo canto de amor a Stalingrado."
The theme of both poems is praise for the Russian city,
which withstood Nazi attacks during World War II.

The "Nuevo canto de amor a Stalingrado," for its
rhythm and predominantly consonant rhyme achieves a per-
suasive rhetorical intensity:

> I touched with these hands the shirt
> of twilight, blue and defeated,
> now I touch the dawning of life
> born with the sun of Stalingrad.

> Yo toqué con mis manos la camisa
> del crepúsculo azul y derrotado
> ahora toco el alba de la vida
> naciendo con el sol de Stalingrado [OC 277].

A critic has maintained that the poems of the first two
Residencias convey to us the idea of the "collage" of modern
painting. [10] By using a similar analogy, we might say that
the poems of España en el corazón, and those dedicated to
Stalingrad, are closer to the murals of the Mexican Revolution because of their inspiration in the people's struggle for
justice.   They introduce the political themes which will receive their maximum lyrical expression in the poems of the
Canto general.

III

THE CANTO GENERAL

The Canto general, written between 1938 and 1949, is
a collection of poems expressing a clear political orientation.
As such, it represents the new aesthetic of Pablo Neruda,
reflected in a poetry that has little to do with what he wrote
prior to "Reunión bajo las nuevas banderas." The thematic
unity of the book, however, is not simply an ideological one.
It is maintained throughout by the primacy he gives to America, as it was in 1400, and as it evolved to the present.
The United States, being for the poet an imperialist nation,
is excluded for the most part.

Chile is the inspiration for most of the poems, and
occupies a central place in the book. The Canto general
began as an epic poem about Chile, the "Canto general de
Chile," and it was not until 1945, when Neruda joined the
Communist Party and was elected senator, that he decided to
extend it to include the whole of Hispanic America. By this
time Neruda had been in Mexico and had visited Machu Picchu
in Peru. The American continent began to fascinate him and
he resolved to write about it.

Neruda dedicated most of his time to being poet and
politician, trying to complete the Canto general while at the
same time engaging in parliamentary debates. But his political activism hindered his poetic creation. Aware of this,
early in 1947, the Communist Party relieved him of his sena-
torial duties and gave him a leave of absence of a year so
that he could finish the Canto. In it, Neruda was to reflect
some of the party's basic ideological tenets. But to think that
the contents of the book are purely propagandistic is to un-
dervalue one of Neruda's most important contributions as a
poet.

By the end of 1947, however, Neruda's activism in-

46

creased.   On November 27,   he published in the Venezuelan
newspaper El Nacional de Caracas his "Carta íntima para
millones de hombres, " in which he took the side of striking
copper miners from northern Chile and publicly denounced
Gabriel González Videla, president of Chile from 1946 to
1952.   As a result, President González Videla brought suit
against him, and on February 3, 1948, the Supreme Appellate
Court of Santiago found the poet guilty and had an order issued
for his arrest.   With the outlawing of the Communist Party
in the same year, Neruda lost his senate seat and so as not
to be jailed, remained a fugitive for a year.   During this
time, he finished the Canto general, divided into 15 sections
and published in 1950.[1]

The Canto general presents the encounter of the American man with his history; the history of an immense and mysterious world with tropical vegetation, great rivers, lofty
mountains, and innumerable wild animals.   We witness the
arrival of the "Conquistadores, " represented by the priest,
the administrator, and the soldier, all of whom cheer for
God, king and country.   But little by little their voices combine in unison and we hear them chanting in praise of gold.
The conquering Spaniards represent a type of antihero dedicated to violence and destruction.   Neruda defends the aborigines, and recalls their uprisings suppressed in blood.   The
wars of independence come next and we get to know the "libertadores" of the American soil.   Social and political conflicts plaguing Latin America from the days of independence
are depicted, and we meet the ruthless "caudillos" and dictators who stand in the way of progress and freedom.   Over
one half of the book is devoted to the present state of affairs
in Latin America.

In spite of the political themes of the Canto general,
its origins were in no way connected with the Chilean Communist Party.   Actually, the first poem of the book was written on May 7, 1938, seven years before Neruda became a
Marxist, and on the occasion of his father's death.   The poem
later formed part of Section III of the Canto, "Los conquistadores. "[2]

From that date, the Canto general began to take shape
in various location of Latin America: in Mexico, where Neruda met the great muralists; in Machu Picchu, where he
saw, as in a vision, the entire history of the American continent unfolding before him; in a number of cities he visited;

and in places where he hid to avoid imprisonment. Nevertheless, the poet's most intensive production occurred between
1948 and 1949, the year he was a fugitive and had to cross
the Andes to seek political asylum in Argentina. The book
was finally published in Mexico on April 3, 1950. The muralist David Alfaro Siqueiros and painter Diego Rivera were
responsible for the illustrations: Siqueiros painted a symbolic springtime of bliss; Rivera, the powerful awakening of the
American race, no longer bound to old Spain. [3]

The Canto general has been called the true epic poem
of the American continent, the true "cantar de gesta," as Alfredo Cardona Peña has defined it. [4] Its political and social
themes clearly show the poet's preferences, and as it happened in España en el corazón, they tend to make some of
its parts prosaic and some verse commonplace. Yet, it is
precisely these themes which inspire meaningful poems, as
we shall see when we analyze some sections of the book in
detail.

Today's critics have chosen as the most powerful parts
of the Canto the poems of "Alturas de Machu Picchu," and
those of the "Canto general de Chile." [5] To these, we may
add the poems dealing with personal reminiscences of childhood, with political persecution, and with human solidarity:
"El fugitivo," and "Yo soy"; as well as the ones dealing with
the ocean and the wonders of its aquatic vegetation in "El
gran océano."

The Canto general begins with "La lámpara en la tierra," a collection of six poems which represents the genesis
of the entire book. The title is symbolic of light on earth.
It is an illumination which reveals the creation of a virgin
continent before the arrival of the "Discoverers." Perhaps
it is for this reason that the poet chooses the year 1400 to
begin his long narrative. His description of America first
gives us a glimpse of the land, its vegetation, the bird and
other animals typical of the southern regions of the Western
Hemisphere, and finally, man. The new continent still does
not have a name, but its vastness and unity is represented
by the combination of two images: "the Incan sediment" ("el
légamo incaico") and "the zapotec flowers" ("las flores zapo-
tecas"), which point to the south and north of the Latin American territorial extension.

In "Los hombres," which concludes "La lámpara en
la tierra," we come face to face with the American men: the

Caribs, Aztecs, Toltecs, Chibchas, Incas, Araucanos, Tupí-
Guaraní, and all the others who inhabited the land.   With
forceful poetic imagery Neruda depicts the American race:

> Like a cup of clay was
> the mineral race: man
> made of stones and atmosphere,
> clean as a bassoon and resonant.
> The moon massaged the Caribs,
> extracted sacred oxygen,
> crushed flowers and roots.
> The men of the islands
> weaved branches and wreaths
> of varicolored sulphur,
> blowing Triton, the mariner,
> on the foamy shores.

> Como la copa de la arcilla era
> la raza mineral, el hombre
> hecho de piedras y atmósfera,
> limpio como los cántaros, sonoro.
> La luna amasó a los caribes,
> extrajo oxígeno sagrado,
> machacó flores y raíces.
> Anduvo el hombre de las islas
> tejiendo ramos y guirnaldas
> de polymitas azufradas,
> y soplando el tritón marino
> en la orilla de las espumas [OC 307-8].

"La lámpara en la tierra" represents the setting from
which the entire history of America unfolds.   In this section,
the poet uses the traditional verse that will be repeated
throughout the Canto general--the hendecasyllable and the
heptasyllable without rhyme.   Neruda's end is to synthesize
the poetic world he creates in metaphors that are no longer
a unique definition of the reality he is representing.   We
need an accumulation of them in order to have a complete
representation of the object he wants to portray.   For example, in "Vienen los pájaros," Neruda calls the eagle an "as-
sassin king" ("el cóndor, rey asesino").   But this is not
enough for the poet, and he adds:

> Solitary cleric of the sky,
> black talisman of the snow,
> hurricane of the falconry.

> fraile solitario del cielo,
> talismán negro de la nieve,
> huracán de la cetrería [OC 301].

This accumulation of images will be the predominant technique used in the book.

The social and political themes of the Canto, which were only implied in "La lámpara en la tierra," in poems such as "Minerales," and which are hardly present in "Canto general de Chile" and in "El gran océano," are expressed clearly in every other section of the book. These themes are reflected in the poet's condemnation of Spain and of corrupt Latin American presidents and dictators, as well as in his attempt to interpret the history of America, and in his pleas for social justice.

In "Alturas de Machu Picchu" Neruda takes a journey backward in time, to give meaning to images and symbols which had been preserved in the Inca ruins. From the heights of Machu Picchu the poet attempts to interpret and, at the same time vindicate, the American tradition. His search for contact with the aborigines and for an understanding of their culture leads him to pre-Hispanic America. It seemed to him that in this period he could find the essential meaning of life: a meaning which transcended blood ties and clans, upheld the brotherhood of man, and preserved a sense of unity embracing not only mankind, but all living things. For now it was no longer a question of the poet's giving expression to his own lyrical experience of life. It was also a question of bringing back to contemporary man some consciousness of the pre-Hispanic man, without which, according to Neruda, life would be thwarted and incomplete. "Alturas de Machu Picchu" will be analyzed in detail in the next chapter because it represents a synthesis of the entire Canto, and because it is essential in explaining Neruda's evolution as a poet committed to an ideology and to social justice.

In the next three sections of the Canto general, "Los conquistadores," "Los libertadores," and "La arena traicionada," the social and political themes become a means of expressing the poet's anti-Spanish sentiment: Neruda records the crimes perpetrated by the colonizers against the aborigines. His vision is that of a chronicler who reports in a journalistic fashion the conquest, the liberation, and the eventual betrayal of America at the hands of government officials more interested in their own gains than in their country. Spain is condemned for colonizing and corrupting the New World.

Neruda begins the first poem of "Los conquistadores"
with the verse: "the butchers destroyed the islands" ("Los
carniceros desolaron las islas"), which immediately points
to a prior judgment he has made of the Spaniards.   The central theme of the "Black Legend" introduced by Bartolomé de
las Casas is repeated by Neruda, to show that the conquest
was a crime against the inhabitants of the American continent.   The aborigines, bound by a spirit of fraternity, are
lauded for fighting bravely against the invaders in a struggle
for survival.

Neruda portrays as disreputable figures all the "conquistadores," from Hernán Cortés to Francisco Pizarro, from
Diego de Almagro to Pedro de Valdivia.   The poet's verses
become slanted, and Neruda inevitably falls into the same
prosaic trap that diminished the literary merits of España en
el corazón.   He becomes more direct in his accusations:

> Cursed by dog and man,
> the infamous wail of the primitive
> jungle, the mountain pass,
> and the waylaying bandit's step.

> Maldito sean perro y hombre
> el aullido infame de la selva
> original, el acechante
> paso de hierro y del bandido [OC 331].

He sadly states that after the conquest:

> Only bones were left
> rigidly placed
> in the form of a cross, for the greatest
> glory of God, and of man.

> Sólo quedaban huesos
> rígidamente colocados
> en la forma de cruz, para mayor
> gloria de Dios y de los hombres [OC 325]

The ironic tone of these last verses is another characteristic
that is repeated in this poetry of social and political protest.

Only two conquistadors escape the designation "exter-
minator" given by Neruda to all the others: Vasco Núñez de
Balboa, who in 1511 became the Governor ad interim of La
Isla Española (Hispaniola), and Alonso de Ercilla y Zúñega,

who composed· "La Araucana," considered to be the best
Spanish epic poem of the 16th century.   Balboa was praised
because he defied the repressive laws of the Spaniards with
regard to the Indians; Ercilla, for singing the great deeds of
the Araucanians, especially the bravery of Lautaro and Caupolicán, and the wisdom of the old chieftain Colocolo.   Neruda
also lauds Ercilla for ignoring the name of Diego Hurtado de
Mendoza, commander of the Spanish troops upon Pedro de
Valdivia's death, and Ercilla's enemy.

Most of the poems in "Los conquistadores" deal with
the conquest of Chile.   It is evident that Neruda is not describing it objectively, and that he used information more legendary than historical.   Nevertheless, he interpreted the sub-
jugation of the Araucanians with stark realism.   It was a
fight that began in 1535 and lasted three centuries.   After innumerable battles, the independence of Chile was achieved.
But the country fell prey to corrupt oligarchies.   Chilean
generals were decorated for assassinating the legitimate heirs
to Lautaro, Caupolicán, and Tucapel.   The last punitive expeditions against the aborigines were waged at the end of the
19th century, when the Araucanians finally had to accept
Chilean rule.   Neruda closes this section with an optimistic
note.   Although the despots won, "Light came in spite of
daggers" ("la luz vino a pesar de los puñales") (OC 352).

In "Los libertadores," sustaining the same political
themes and the same antagonism toward Spain which characterized "Los conquistadores," Neruda gives us a lyrical
exaltation of the liberators of the American soil.   The more
meaningful poems of this section are the ones dedicated to
Lautaro, O'Higgins, San Martín, and Miranda, in which the
historical vision predominates.   "Los libertadores" is supe-
rior to "Los conquistadores" because it conveys Neruda's political message while it leaves out the propaganda, and because at the same time it displays an admirable variety of
metrical patterns.   Most of this section is written in verses
of eight and 11 syllables.   In one instance, in the "Antiestro-
fa" of the poem dedicated to José Miguel Carrera, Neruda
tries to reproduce the rhythm of the classical hexameter, as
had Rubén Darío in the poem "Salutación del optimista."

As an introduction, Neruda begins "Los libertadores"
with a symbolic image of a tree, cut at the base by the various wars fought against the Spaniards, but which, in spite of
its wounds, regenerates many leaves.   Each new leaf gives
birth to a liberator.

The first two names to appear are those of Cuauhtémoc,
the Aztec leader who replaced Moctezuma after the latter died,
and who fought bravely against Cortés, and Fray Bartolomé de
las Casas, who denounced the Spanish maltreatment of the Indians.   Cuauhtémoc is called by Neruda "young brother."
Bartolomé de las Casas is referred to as the white spiritual
father who devoted his life to attaining for his people a state
of peaceful coexistence with the Indians.

The conquest of Chile is the subject of the next nine
poems of this section, and Lautaro appears as the most important historical figure:

> The blood touches a corridor of quartz.
> The rock grows where the drop of water falls.
> Thus Lautaro is brought to life from the earth.

> La sangre toca un corredor de cuarzo.
> La piedra crece donde cae la gota.
> Así nace Lautaro de la tierra [OC 364].

Tribute is paid to the Araucanian leader who joined Pedro de
Valdivia only to betray the Spaniards later.

The poems that deal with the conquest of Chile are followed by an "Intermedio," which separates conquered America
from liberated America.   After the "Intermedio," the poems
which because of their lyrical excellence deserve a closer look
are those dedicated to Bernardo O'Higgins, the liberator of
Chile, José de San Martín, who with Simón Bolívar liberated
South America, and Francisco Miranda, Bolívar's precursor
in the Venezuelan movement for independence.

In eulogizing the three liberators, Neruda is at the
same time eulogizing their fatherland.   The poet's love for
the Chilean hero is expressed in these verses:

> You are Chile, betwixt patriarch and horseman.
> . . .
> But we have inherited your courage,
> your inalterable silent heart,
> your indestructible fatherly posture;
> and you, amid the dazzling avalanche
> of ancient hussars, amid agile
> uniforms blue and honey colored,
> are with us today, the father
> of our people, an immutable soldier.

Eres Chile, entre patricarca y huaso.
...
Pero hemos heredado tu firmeza,
tu inalterable corazón callado,
tu indestructible posición paterna,
y tú, entre la avalancha cegadora,
de húsares del pasado, entre los agiles
uniformes azules y dorados,
estás hoy con nosotros, eres nuestro
padre del pueblo, inmutable soldado [OC 377, 379].

Neruda then glorifies San Martín for his role in liberating
Latin America from the Spanish yoke.   Using the elements of
nature to create poetic images, the poet gives us a description of the Argentinian leader which is lyrical and suggestive:

San Martín, other captains
will glitter more than you, wearing their
          embroidered
vine leaves of luminous salt,
and will continue to talk like cascades,
but there is not another like you, dressed with
earth and solitude, snow and clover,
We find you where the river turns back,
we salute you in the agrarian way
of the flourishing Tucumanian,
and, lifting your vestments, oh dusty father,
we come across you on the road and on horseback.

San Martín, otros capitanes
fulgurarán más que tú, llevan bordados
sus pámpanos de sal fosforescente,
otros hablan aún como cascadas,
pero no hay uno como tú, vestido
de tierra y soledad, de nieve y trébol.
Te encontramos al retornar del río,
te saludamos en la forma agraria
de la Tucumania florida,
y en los caminos, a caballo
te cruzamos corriendo y levantando
tu vestidura, padre polvoriento [OC 381].

Turning to Miranda, Neruda composes an elegy, without using punctuation, with images that accentuate the fog and
the cold of death:

they lower him with rope into the damp

enemy land no one salutes it is cold
it is the cold of the tomb in Europe.

lo bajan con cordeles a la mojada
tierra enemiga nadie saluda hace frío
hace frío de tumba en Europa [OC 385].

Miranda had been the first to instigate revolution in Latin
America, but had died without laurels and without recognition.

Neruda closes this section of the Canto general paying
tribute to all the liberators in "Llegará el día." The death
of each liberator is cause for rejoicing because it represents
the seed for a new American life.

In "La arena traicionada" Neruda condemns all the
traitors of the American soil. The brief introduction to this
section speaks of the henchmen and the oppressors, whom the
poet calls "hijos terribles con venenosa leche de serpiente"
(OC 429). In this violent chapter of the history of America,
Neruda accuses those who have set up antidemocratic re-
gimes. Alongside Juan Manuel de Rosas, García Moreno and
Rodríguez Francia, President González Videla, who in 1946
had been elected with the help of the leftist parties but two
years later had abolished the Chilean Left, comes under
heaviest criticism. Neruda denounces imperialistic organizations and the foreign capitalists who exploit the wealth of
America. He, then, turns against those writers who have
remained aloof in their "celestial" literature, striving to
achieve "art for art's sake," while forgetting their duties to
the people. Using a very subjective tone, the poet questions
the worth of so many imitators in "Los poetas celestes":

> What were you doing, you Gideists,
> intellectuals, Rilkeists,
> mystics, false existential
> conjurers, surrealist
> poppies lighted
> in a tomb, Europeanized
> cadavers of fashion ...
> ...
> You weren't doing anything but escaping:
> you were selling stacked-up rubbish,
> you were searching for celestial hair,
> fearful plants, broken fingernails,
> "pure form," "sorcery,"
> ...

without seeing the agonizing stone,
without defending, without conquering,
blinder than the garlands
of the cemetery, when rain
falls over the immobile
rotten flowers of the tomb.

¿Qué hicisteis vosotros, gidistas,
intelectualistas, rilkistas,
misterizantes, falsos brujos
existenciales, amapolas
surrealistas encendidas
en una tumba, europeizados
cadáveres de la moda ...
. . .
No hicisteis nada sino la fuga:
vendisteis hacinado detritus,
buscasteis cabellos celestes,
plantas cobardes, uñas rotas,
"Belleza pura, " "sortilegio, "
. . .
sin ver la piedra en egonía,
sin defender, sin conquistar,
más ciegos que las coronas
del cementerio, cuando cae
la lluvia sobre las inmóviles
flores podridas de las tumbas [OC 446-7].

Before "Reunión bajo las nuevas banderas, " of course, Neruda himself had repeatedly used the image of the poppy, and
had found refuge in the humid tombs of graveyards. By re-
jecting "los poetas celestes, " Neruda implies a rejection of
his own poetry prior to his engagement with social realism.
Now the poet feels closer to the people and encounters meaning in life. He is even willing to reply to that which his
brothers ask of him:

And what did you do? Didn't your work come
to help the poor miner,
to assuage the pain of those betrayed,
didn't the syllable of fire come to you
to cry out and defend your people?

¿Tú qué hiciste? ¿No vino tu palabra
para el hermano de las bajas minas,
para el dolor de los traicionados,
no vino a tí la sílaba de llamas
para clamar y defender tu pueblo? [OC 478].

The answer to these questions is in the poem "Acuso,"
which has the same title as a political discourse against González Videla, pronounced by Neruda in the Chilean Senate a
few months before he lost his seat.   The harshness of the
poem is intensified by the political message:

> I, then, accused the one
> who had strangled hope,
> I called every corner of America
> and I placed his name in the cave
> of the dishonored.
>   Then, the sellouts
> and the ones wallowing in corruption
> reproached me for their pack of crimes:
> government secretaries, police,
> they recorded in grease
> their unkempt insults about me;
> but the walls were watching
> when the traitors wrote my name
> in capital letters; and the night,
> with its innumerable hands,
> nocturnal hands of the people,
> was erasing the disgrace with which they,
> in vain, wanted to stain my verse.
> . . .
> But mine is a living word,
> and my free heart accuses.

> Acusé entonces al que había
> estrangulado la esperanza,
> llamé a los rincones de América
> y puse su nombre en la cueva
> de las deshonras.
>   Entonces crímenes
> me reprocharon la jauría
> de los vendidos y alquilados:
> los secretarios del gobierno,
> los policías, escribieron
> con alquitrán su espeso insulto
> contra mí, pero las paredes
> miraban cuando los traidores
> escribían con grandes letras
> mi nombre, y la noche borraba,
> con sus manos innumerables,
> manos del pueblo y de la noche,
> la ignominia que vanamente
> quieren arrojar a mi canto.

...
Pero mi palabra está viva,
y mi libre corazón acusa [OC 478-9].

Neruda is here accusing the President of Chile, whom he
does not mention by name, and the unfair trial he received
in Santiago as a result of the President's meddling with the
judges.

"González Videla el traidor de Chile" is the last poem
of "La arena traicionada, " and it is inferior to the other
poems included in this section.   It is a prosaic diatribe that
sounds like a propagandistic speech:

In my country vileness governs.

González Videla is the rat who shook
his filthy hair, full of manure and blood,
over my land which he betrayed.   Each day
he takes from his pockets the stolen coins
and thinks whether tomorrow he shall sell
         territory
or blood.

En mi patria preside la vileza.

Es González Videla la rata que sacude
su pelambrera llena de estiércol y de sangre
sobre la tierra mía que vendió.   Cada día
saca de sus bolsillos las monedas robadas
y piensa si mañana venderá territorio
o sangre [OC 480].

In this section of the Canto general we have a poetry
of accusation rooted in political ideology.   The language used
by Neruda is very strong and becomes soft and lyrical only
when the poet suggests, with visual images, some aspect of
the American landscape.

The 18 short poems included in "América, no invoco
tu nombre en vano, " represent a lyrical synthesis of the preceding five sections of the Canto general.   But from this point
on, the apparent epic tone of the book is substituted by a more
personal tone, and the poet becomes the sole interpreter of
historical facts and autobiographical data.   As a result, the
Canto general turns more and more into a "canto personal. "
In "Centro América" and "América" Neruda gives us images

which, while describing the landscape, also relate to the social drama unfolding before us in Latin America, as interpreted by the poet.

Neruda begins to identify himself with America, but
not any longer in a metaphysical or cosmic way, rather, ma-
terially and taking into consideration the reality that sur-
rounds him.   The social and political themes in this section
are expressed in the poems, "Un asesino duerme," "Los
crímenes," "Los dictadores," "Hambre en el sur," and
"América." Most of the other compositions deal with a description of the American soil.   The poet concludes this section exclaiming:

> America, I don't invoke your name in vain.
> When I subject to the heart the blade,
> when I endure in my soul the dripping,
> when through the windows
> a new day penetrates me,
> I exist and I dwell in the light that
>   gives me being,
> I live in the shadow that determines me,
> I sleep and I awake in your essential dawn:
> sweet like grapes, and terrible,
> conductor of sugar and punishment,
> drenched in the semen of your species,
> suckled in the blood of your heritage.

> América, no invoco tu nombre en vano.
> Cuando sujeto al corazón la espada,
> cuando aguanto en el alma la gotera,
> cuando por las ventanas
> un nuevo día tuyo me penetra,
> soy y estoy en la luz que me produce,
> vivo en la sombra que me determina,
> duermo y despierto en tu esencial aurora:
> dulce como las uvas, y terrible,
> conductor del azúcar y el castigo,
> empapado en esperma de tu especie,
> amamantado en sangre de tu herencia
>   [OC 490].

From this poem on, Neruda will no longer make a distinction
between epic and lyric poetry, as Rodríguez Monegal has
pointed out, between narrative and evocative poetry, between
"canto" and "cuento."[6]

The "Canto general de Chile" is a lyrical song with a
highly personal tone and a specific local habitation, the south
of Chile.   As such, it forms a kind of interval between the
first part of the book and the poems that follow, since the social and political themes are hardly present in this section.
What characterizes these poems is a series of portraits: the
south of Chile wet by constant rainfalls; the naked green ocean;
the thunder and the snowy-white splendor of the Cordillera de
los Andes; the small industries which thrive in secondary cities and towns.   The principal theme in "Canto general de
Chile" is love for nature and for the Chilean landscape, as
we can see in poems such as "Eternidad," "Jinete en la
lluvia," "Mares de Chile," or in "Oda al río Mapocho."
Neruda also finds the occasion to pay homage to four Chilean
friends: Tomás Lago, collaborator with Neruda in Anillos
(1926); Rubén Azócar, a Chilean novelist who wrote on the
Archipelago of Chiloé (southern Chile); Juvencio Valle, a contemporary poet; and Diego Muñoz, a novelist and short story
writer.

The social themes, much more than the political ones,
are emphasized in "La tierra se llama Juan."   The heroes
are the manual workers, and Neruda tells us their life history, their sufferings and hopes.   The poet abandons the rhe-
toric so evident in his poetry with political orientation and
greatly simplifies his style, using the language of the common man to reach the common man.   What we have in this
section is a kind of newspaper reporting in verse.   The pro-
tagonists are the humble workers: carpenters, shoemakers,
miners, and thousands of unknown comrades who work for
their families and country and more often than not are ex-
ploited by what the poet characterizes as inhuman capitalist
organizations.

The first poem of "La tierra se llama Juan" is dedicated to Cristóbal Miranda, a ditch-digger whom the poet
knew.   Jesús Gutiérrez, a farmer, tells us that his father
died in Monterrey; Luis Cortés, who suffered at the hands of
the police, describes his imprisonment:

> They pushed me to Pisagua.
> You know, comrade, how that is.
> Many became ill, others
> went mad ...
>
> Me tiraron a Pisagua.
> Usted sabe, camarada, como es eso.

Muchos cayeron enfermos, otros
enloquecieron ... [OC 517].

Olegario Sepúlveda, a shoemaker, says:

I am a cobbler in Talcahuano.
Sepúlveda, across from the Great Dam.
Any time, sir, we, the poor,
never close our door.

Soy zapatero en Talcahuano.
Sepúlveda, frente al Dique grande.
Cuando quiera, señor, los pobres
nunca cerramos la puerta [OC 519].

Arturo Carrión, a sailor, writes to his wife from prison,
asking her to send him a new shirt and some tobacco. Abraham Jesús Brito, a popular poet--as opposed to the "poetas
celestes"--is paid tribute because he is very poor but at the
same time makes those who hear his lyrical verses rejoice.

With somber descriptions, Neruda gives us an account
of the miserable living conditions in the silver mines of Boli-
via and in the copper mines of Chile. The poem "La tierra
se llama Juan" synthesizes the essence of the entire section.
Juan is not only the name given to the land, but it also
stands for every unnamed worker in the most remote parts of
Latin America:

His bones are everywhere.
But he lives. He returned from earth. He
was born.
He was reborn like an everlasting plant.

Sus huesos están en todas partes.
Pero vive. Regresó de la tierra. Ha nacido.
Ha nacido de nuevo como una planta eterna
[OC 531].

The poem ends with Neruda's denunciation of social conditions in Latin America, his exhortation to the workers to unite
in the fight to improve their lots, and once again, a note of
optimism that all this will be achieved.

The political themes are taken up by Neruda again in
"Que despierte el leñador." The poet urges the America of
the aborigines not to give up her identity and to resist the

political, social, economic, and cultural imperialism imposed
by the "Colossus of the North." Abraham Lincoln, to whom
the title "Que despierte el leñador" refers, is recalled to
life.

Neruda shows in these poems mixed feelings of admi-
ration and dislike, affection and hate. He states that he is
on the side of the American people, and praises Lincoln, Mel-
ville, Whitman, Poe, Lockridge, Thomas Wolfe, and Norman
Mailer. He defends Howard Fast and attacks the press, especially the Hearst column, Time and Newsweek. His verses
become more violent and he attacks the U.S. imperialism.
If North America attempts to destroy the Indian heritage of
the South, then Neruda tells us that he must speak out:

> We shall emerge from stones and air
> to bite you:
> we shall emerge from the last window
> to throw fire at you:
> we shall emerge from the deepest waves
> to pierce you with thorns:
> we shall emerge from the furrows so that the seed
> will hit you like a Colombian fist,
>
> we shall emerge to deny you bread and water
> we shall emerge to burn you in hell.
>
> Saldremos de las piedras y del aire
> para morderte:
> saldremos de la última ventana
> para volcarte fuego:
> saldremos de las olas más profundas
> para clavarte con espinas:
> saldremos del surco para que la semilla
> golpee como un puño colombiano,
>
> saldremos para negarte el pan y el agua
> saldremos para quemarte en el infierno
>   [OC 544-5].

And he does so, continuing the political tradition in poetry
that began with Rubén Darío's "Oda a Roosevelt."

Neruda's accusation of the United States is not meant
for the land or the people. It is directed against the indus-
trial monopolies, Wall Street, and colonial and expansionist
policies: "May none of that come to pass" ("Que nada de eso
pase") (OC 548), hopes Neruda.

While being critical of United States government agencies, the poet manifests his love for Abraham Lincoln and for the country to the North.   He wants to bring the hero of the Civil War back to life so that the latter can steer his country on the right course again:

> May the woodcutter awake.
> May Abraham come with his axe
> and his wooden plate
> and eat with the peasants.
>
> Que despierte el leñador.
> Que venga Abraham con su hacha
> y con su plato de madera
> a comer con los campesinos [OC 548].

Lincoln is needed to get rid of the new masters that have taken over in America.

The violence of language is tempered when Neruda sings of the vastness of the northern continent, remembering the wet Northwest, the dry Southwest, and Milwaukee, a city raised against "wind and snow." He tells us that there is a place (he does not name it) west of the Colorado River which he loves, and pays tribute to the rich lands of the Far West. Manhattan and the Hudson River are also eulogized.

Neruda ends "Que despierte el leñador" with a call for peace, although he realizes that the voice of a poet is much weaker than armed troops.   The last three lines close the poem with a cordial note:

> I came to resolve nothing.
> I came here to sing
> and to let you sing with me.
>
> Yo no vengo a resolver nada.
> Yo vine aquí para cantar
> y para que cantes conmigo [OC 550].

The poems of "El fugitivo," "Las flores de Punitaqui," "Los ríos del canto," and "Coral de año nuevo para la patria en tinieblas," deal with various episodes in the life of the poet.   Neruda recounts with anecdotal style his revolutionary activities, always expressing a political point of view.   He feels the need to become identified with the people and expounds on his materialistic philosophy.

In "El fugitivo" Neruda is thankful to the people of Chile who were able to shield him from the persecutions of González Videla and the secret police.   With the help of many Chileans, Neruda was able to cross over the Andes to Argentina and finally reach Mexico.   Many of the poems in this section were written while the poet was escaping from his enemies.

González Videla appears once again as the tyrant, and Neruda closes this short chapter of the Canto denouncing him and trying to achieve complete identification with the people of his country:

> I don't feel alone at night,
> in earth's darkness.
> I am the people, innumerable peoples.
> . . .
> From death we are reborn.
>
> no me siento solo en la noche,
> en la oscuridad de la tierra.
> Soy pueblo, pueblo innumerable.
> . . .
> Desde la muerte renacemos [OC 565-6].

"El fugitivo" ends with the poet's belief that he, together with his people, will experience a rebirth founded on social justice, where there will be no more room for tyrants.

The social and political themes which highlighted the best sections of the Canto general, "Alturas de Machu Picchu" and "La arena traicionada," are repeated in the section, "Las flores de Punitaqui": hunger, strikes, exploitation of the riches of the subsoil, the call to solidarity.   But "Las flores de Punitaqui" is definitely inferior from a stylistic point of view to the rest of the Canto general.

Many of the poems in this section, while expressing a political theme, degenerate into propaganda.   In "El pueblo," for example, Neruda finds himself in the midst of revolutionary people who are carrying red flags:

> The people were carrying their red flags
> and I was among them, in the stone they
>   touched,
> in the thundering day's journey,
> in the high songs of struggle.

Paseaba el pueblo sus banderas rojas
y entre ellos en la piedra que tocaron
estuve en la jornada fragorosa
y en las altas canciones de la lucha
    [OC 578].

The poem ends with the people marching to victory and wav-
ing their red flags.

Commitment to an ideology can be justified by rational
argumentation, but the substitution of propaganda for poetry
cannot.   Other poems in this section are weakened by the
same ideological bias, as we see in "La huelga" and "El camino de oro. " In "El poeta, " Neruda once again rejects the
poetry of death he wrote prior to his political conversion.

"Los ríos del canto" is dedicated to poets and musi-
cians.   Neruda sends messages of warmth and gratitude to
friends he met in Europe and in other countries of Latin
America.   He is especially indebted to those who were kind
to him when he was in need and those who showed him the
way to social justice: Miguel Otero Silva, in Caracas; Rafael
Alberti, in Spain; González Carbalho, in Argentina.   Then the
poet remembers two dead friends, the Mexican musician Silvestre Revueltas and Miguel Hernández, the Spanish poet who
died in a fascist jail.   Paying homage to the Mexican, Neruda
writes:

When such a man as Silvestre Revueltas
returns finally to the soil,
there is a murmur, a wave
of voice and of cries that prepares and
        propagates his departure.
The tiny roots say to the grain:
    "Silvestre has died, "
and the wheat undulates his name in the
        hillsides
and later the bread will know it.
. . .
Ah, but from your name comes music
and from your music, like a marketplace,
come wreaths of fragrant laurel
and apples of fine scent and symmetry.

Cuando un hombre como Silvestre Revueltas
vuelve definitivamente a la tierra
hay un rumor, una ola

de voz y de llanto que prepara y propaga
　　su partida.
Las pequeñas raíces dicen a los cereales:
　　"Murió Silvestre,"
y el trigo ondula su nombre en las laderas
y luego el pan lo sabe.
　. . .
Ah, pero de tu nombre sale música
y de tu música, como de un mercado,
salen coronas de laurel fragrante
y manzanas de olor y simetría [OC 590-1].

Turning to Miguel Hernández, the poet of social consciousness
who he admired so much, Neruda tells him:

Miguel of Spain, star
of satin-flat lands, I shall not forget you,
　　my son,
I shall not forget you, my son.

Miguel de España, estrella
de tierras arrasadas, no te olvido, hijo mío,
no te olvido, hijo mío [OC 594].

The political themes are present in this section, which
like "Las flores de Punitaqui," represents a poetic descent in
the Canto. Neruda refers to Spain as being the wicked Cain.
He speaks of revenge and hails Mao Tse-tung as the spiritual
father of poets:

Miguel, far from the prison in Osuna, far
from cruelty, Mao Tse-tung guides
your tormented poetry in the struggle
toward our victory.

Miguel, lejos de la prisión de Osuna, lejos
de la crueldad, Mao Tse-tung dirige
tu poesía despedazada en el combate
hacia nuestra victoria [OC 593].

In the poem dedicated to Rafael Alberti, Neruda does
not forget to eulogize García Lorca. He also remembers
another social poet, Nicolás Guillén, and speaks of him with
regard in the "Carta a Miguel Otero Silva, en Caracas."
Having paid tribute to his friends, the poet looks to the fatherland from exile.

"Coral de año nuevo para la patria en tinieblas" is a good example of a group of poems of uneven quality, such as we have seen in España en el corazón. The best poems of this section, "Saludo" and "Feliz año para mi patria en tinieblas," are songs to the fatherland, while poems such as "González Videla" and "Los mentirosos" are good examples of propagandistic verse. The social and political themes predominate, although other themes, such as praise for the workers and national heroes, love for the Chilean landscape, and the loneliness of exile, are also present.

In "Saludo," the poet offers a hymn in worship of what he sees:

Fatherland, summer covers your sweet and
        tough body.
Your mountainous borders are tall and blue
like a carbon copy of heaven,
and from there snow has departed
galloping with turbulent lips toward the sea.
Perhaps, at this very moment, you wear the
        green tunic
I adore; forests, water, and wheat in your waist.
Oh marine land, with the sea you move
your iridescent universe of sand and oysters.

Patria, el verano cubre tu cuerpo dulce y duro.
Las aristas de donde se ha marchado la nieve
galopando al océano con labios turbulentos,
se ven azules y altas como carbón del cielo.
Tal vez, a esta hora, llevas la verde túnica
que adoro, bosques, agua, y en la cintura
        el trigo.
Y junto al mar, amada, patria marina, mueves
tu universo irisado de arenas y ostras [OC 595].

In "Feliz año para mi patria en tinieblas," Neruda expresses his longing to return to Chile:

This is a happy year for you, everyone,
and the soil, beloved land of Araucania.
This new night, woods, rivers and roads
keep you and my existence apart.
But my heart gallops as a dark steed
toward you, my humble homeland.

Feliz este año, para ti, para todos

los hombres, y las tierras, Araucanía amada.
Entre tú y mi existencia hay esta noche nueva
que nos separa, y bosques y ríos y caminos.
Pero hacia ti, pequeña patria mía,
como un caballo oscuro mi corazón galopa ...
　　[OC 610].

The context of both poems is familiar: the long journey and the torment of exile are motifs which Neruda exploits
thoroughly and eloquently. His nostalgia for the fatherland is
very subjective. What the poet gives us is a lyrical statement of mood--a mood that grows out of immediate experi-
ence--repeated, qualified, elaborated until it becomes a meta-
phor and finally, a representative state of mind. He conveys
in his own terms the feeling of loss and separation, and his
intention to return.

Neruda abandons the lyrical tone expressed in his
songs of praise for the fatherland and uses imprecatory language in "González Videla" to depict the President of Chile as
a "lying dog" and a "malicious louse." The poem "Los mentirosos" is a diatribe against those civic leaders and politicians who supported González Videla. As with other propagandistic verse, there is no definite context to enrich the meaning
of these poems and Neruda reexamines old concerns without
contributing anything new in technique or perspective. It is
unfortunate that these last two poems overshadow Neruda's
celebration of love for Chile in this section of the Canto general.

The last two sections of the book, "El gran océano" and
"Yo soy," deal with a poetry of vision and objectivity and a
poetry of analysis and subjectivity, respectively. The poems
of "El gran océano" give us a visual experience of the sea,
and they begin and end at the side of the sea. The poems of
"Yo soy" are an analysis of Neruda's own life, as a poet and
as a man committed to a political ideology. Both sections
presuppose a correspondence between the outer world and the
inner world of the poet. Before "Reunión bajo las nuevas banderas" such as correspondence was absurd, but now the poet
has found a meaningful relationship with the reality that sur-
rounds him. His love for the sea makes such a relationship
even more harmonious.

Even though on more than one occasion Neruda has repudiated his poetry written before the beginning of the Spanish
Civil War, in "El gran océano" he does not reject his old me-

taphysical themes: the union of man with nature; the concern for time and its destructive qualities; the mystery of the sea; and death. In spite of his insistence on adhering to the tenets of social realism, the poems of "El gran océano" demonstrate that the surrealist poet of <u>Residencia en la tierra</u> is by no means dead.

Although the social themes are present in poems such as "Los hijos de la costa, " and "Los puertos, " the central theme of "El gran océano" is the formation of the ocean and its incessant movement, which are symbolic of man's permanence and of eternity. From this section of the <u>Canto general</u> Neruda emerges as the lyrical poet of the sea. No themes which can be related to the ocean are left out. The sea is represented as metaphysically united to the destiny of man.

Using images and epithets which, as John H. R. Polt has pointed out, are typical of the baroque poetry of Luis de Góngora, Neruda describes the birth of the ocean:[7]

> When the stars changed into
> earth and metal, silencing
> energy, and the cup of dawn
> and carbons was overturned,
> then the sea, submerging the
> bonfire in its royal colors,
> fell like a burning drop from
> distance to distance, from hour to hour:
> its blue fire changed into sphere,
> the air of its wheel became a bell,
> its essential spirit trembled in foam,
> and in the light of salt the flower
> of its spacious autonomy was lifted.
> . . .
> the limy amaranth flower grew.

> Cuando se trasmutaron las estrellas
> en la tierra y en metal, cuando apagaron
> la energía y volcada fue la copa
> de auroras y carbones, sumergida
> la hoguera en sus moradas,
> el mar cayó como una gota ardiendo
> de distancia en distancia, de hora en hora:
> su fuego azul se convirtió en esfera,
> el aire de sus ruedas fue campana,
> su interior esencial tembló en la espuma,
> y en la luz de la sal fue levantada

la flor de su espaciosa autonomía.
...
creció la flor calcárea de amaranto
    [OC 613-5f].

But for the poet these images are not enough, and he adds a
series of epithets to complete his description:

Everything was life, tremulous substance,
carnivorous petals that bit,
an accumulated nude quantity,
throbbings of seminal plants,
bleeding of humid sphere,
a perpetual blue wind that demolished
the sudden limits of being.
Thus the immobile light became a mouth
and bit the royal purple jewels.
The less firm form was the ocean,
the translucid grotto of life,
the existential mass, glider of
bunches, fabrics of ovary,
the germinal teeth spilled,
the swords of the matutinal serum,
the common organs of union:
everything in you throbbed filling
the water with cavities and shudder.

Todo era ser, substancia temblorosa,
pétalos carniceros que mordían,
acumulada cantidad desnuda,
palpitaciones de plantas seminales,
sangría de la húmeda esfera,
perpetuo viento azul que derribaba
los límites abruptos de los seres.
Y así la luz inmóvil fue una boca
y mordió su morada pedrería.
Fue océano la forma menos dura,
la translúcida gruta de la vida,
la masa existencial, deslizadora
de racimos, las telas del ovario,
los germinales dientes derramados,
las espadas del suero matutino,
los órganos acervos del enlace:
todo en ti palpitó llenando el agua
de cavidades y estremecimientos [OC 615].

The political themes are absent in this section of the

Canto general. Using images and sounds that evoke the best
periods of baroque poetry in the Spanish language, Neruda
abandons the apparently simple course of the book. The message in most of the poems is an appraisal of marine life and
of the sea. Neruda colors saltwater snails, shellfish, and
molluscs with different hues, and depicts the birds of the sea
wandering along the coasts. Other descriptive passages deal
with detailed accounts of underwater life, of exotic places po-
pulated with men of stone, of archeological mysteries. His
love songs, "A una estatua de proa" and "Rapa Nui," are
filled with laughter and sunlight.

The best poems of "El gran océano" are: "Molluscas
gongorinas," in which Neruda uses baroque images that stand
in apparent contradiction to the materialistic creed he pro-
fesses; "La ola," with its musical hendecasyllable verse which
imitates the movement of the waves; "A una estatua de proa,"
whose title reveals a theme rooted in classical mythology
which symbolizes the seafaring people--mariners, fishermen,
buccaneers; and, "Los enigmas."

"Los enigmas" is a philosophical poem which poses
many questions. Neruda gives only one answer to them: "el
mar lo sabe," the sea knows because the sea is a depository
of all the mysteries of the universe. The poet confesses his
own ignorance and comes to the conclusion that man is a cap-
tive of the surrounding reality:

I walked as you did, scratching
the unending star,
and I awoke, naked, in the night,
and found myself caught in a net,
the only fish, contained by the wind.

Anduve como vosotros escarbando
la estrella interminable,
y en mi red, en la noche, me desperté desnudo,
única presa, pez encerrado en el viento
    [OC 637].

The image of the fish imprisoned by the wind suggests that
man awakens from a state of sleep to the world of reality;
soon he realizes, however, that he is contained by it.

The social preoccupation of the poet is expressed with
realistic details in "Los puertos," in which Neruda emphasizes the miserable conditions of many Latin American ports,

Tocopilla, Antofagasta, Iquique, Mollendo, Mazatlán, and Pisagua, among them. He does not idealize these "windows to the sea." Rather, he describes them in sordid terms:

> Oh ports covered with sand, flooded
> with saltpeter and with the secret salt
> which leaves the suffering in the homeland
> and carries the gold to an unknown god
> whose nails scraped the crust
> of our painful territories.

> Oh puertos arenosos, inundados
> por el salitre, por la sal secreta
> que deja los dolores en la patria
> y lleva el oro al dios desconocido
> cuyas uñas rasparon la corteza
> de nuestros dolorosos territorios [OC 629-30].

Pisagua is depicted as a port afflicted by torment in her empty ruins, while Mollendo is a yellow promontory of death.

What characterizes the rest of the poems in this section is a feeling of nostalgia for Chilean ports, where marine life emerges from the immensity of the waters; a mysterious fascination with Rapa Nui and her enormous and unique statues of stone; a preoccupation with death; and a curiosity for the enigmatic relics hidden in the subaquatic world.

"Yo soy" is a poetic statement in which Neruda defines himself primarily as a political being. In the midst of human solidarity, the poet has turned his back on solitude and desolation and has found comfort in the company of poor people.

An intimate nostalgia is the leitmotif of the poems that deal with Neruda's reminiscences of childhood in the distant and rainy south; his long journey throughout the world; the setbacks he encountered in his political and diplomatic careers; the return to the fatherland; the exile to Mexico; and the poet's satisfaction in writing for the humble people.

Two underlying thoughts characterize this poetry of political orientation: an optimistic vision of the world, and a moral commitment to social justice. The social realism used here by Neruda is not merely a literary attitude but also a political doctrine. The poet has faith in his party and joins the people in solidarity with them. He states "soy un buen compañero, " and pledges to work from exile to improve social and political conditions in Chile and in the rest of Latin America.

In "Yo soy," Neruda confesses that his Canto general was generated primarily by a feeling of anger.   But one does not only find wrath and indignation in these pages.   In "La vida," for example, we have a positive force which can be reduced to a feeling of happiness and affability.   Everywhere eternal love blossoms:

> The world
> has the naked color of apples: the rivers
> carry along a wealth of rustic tokens
> and everywhere lives Rosalie the gentle
> and Juan the companion ...

> El mundo
> tiene un color desnudo de manzana: los ríos
> arrastran un caudal de medallas silvestres
> y en toda parte vive Rosalía la dulce
> y Juan el compañero ... [OC 670].

Behind these symbols there is only the void of the past, the void of experience which has now become simple memory, of solitude which time has turned to stone.

Leaving us his poetic statement, Neruda tells us that although some of his roots can be found in classical Spanish poetry, or even in more recent French verse, his present orientation is political and Mayakovsky's social realism sets the guidelines:

> I leave my old books, collected
> throughout the world, venerated
> for their majestic typography,
> to the new poets of America,
>   to those that one day
> will spin the meaning of tomorrow
> in their raucous, interrupting loom.
> ...
> That they see in Mayakovsky how the
>   star ascended
> and ears of corn were born from its rays.

> Dejo mis viejos libros, recogidos
> en rincones del mundo, venerados
> en su tipografía majestuosa,

> a los nuevos poetas de América,
>   a los que un día
> hilarán en el ronco telar interrumpido
> las significaciones de mañana.
>   . . .
> Que en Maiakovsky vean como ascendió
>   la estrella
> y como de sus rayos nacieron las espigas
>   [OC 671-2].

The final verses of "Yo soy" have nothing that is intense or
very poetic:

> Thus ends this book, here I leave you
> my Canto general, written during
> persecution, sung beneath
> the clandestine wings of my homeland.
> Today, the fifth of February, in this year
> of 1949, in Chile, in "Godomar
> de Chena, " a few months before
> the forty-fifth year of my age.

> Así termina este libro, aquí dejo
> mi Canto general, escrito
> en la persecución, cantando bajo
> las alas clandestinas de mi patria.
> Hoy 5 de febrero, en este año
> de 1949, en Chile, en "Godomar
> de Chena, " algunos meses antes
> de los cuarenta y cinco de mi edad [OC 675].

The book, viewed as a whole, illustrates what is perhaps the most exciting attribute of Neruda's genius: his ability to capture the mood of a current historical moment
through images that evoke the history of his race; or, stated
another way, his ability to express a contemporary state of
mind in terms of the enduring qualities that define his nation--
its landscape, its tangible and legendary past.

As a social poet waging his fight on behalf of the
"have-nots, " Neruda is masterful. It is sufficient to read
"Alturas de Machu Picchu, " as we shall see in the next chapter, to be convinced of this. As his themes become more
social and political, his poetry becomes more comprehensible.
Images and metaphors are not so abundant as in his earlier
books, and become clearer. The poet's preoccupation with
death has been abandoned for a universal preoccupation with
man's faith.

Reading the Canto general, it is evident that Communism has played an important role in the poet's attitude, and his cry is for social justice. But even when Neruda becomes politically active this does not mean that he stops being a poet. There are details in his poetry which can be suppressed without a loss, such as the propagandistic verse. But these details do not make up the essence of his writings. Whenever his concepts form an organic part of his poetry, the propaganda ends and the poetry dominates.

The political and social themes of the Canto general, one of the 20th century's major poetic compositions in any language, are a direct result of Neruda's involvement with Marxism. In the evolution of the poet, the Canto general represents a logical sequence of "Reunión bajo las nuevas banderas," and España en el corazón.

IV

ALTURAS DE MACHU PICCHU

Section II of the Canto general, "Alturas de Machu
Picchu," is a political and historical interpretation of America.   The lost city of the Incas[1] serves as the setting which
symbolizes the destiny of the American man, from his beginning to the present.   As a man committed to a political ideology, the poet has a definite set of norms to follow, a system
of values that looks to social revolution as a base from which
to change the world.   "Alturas de Machu Picchu" reflects the
social and political themes in the poetry of Pablo Neruda.

To understand the total message of this section of the
Canto general, it is important to consider some biographical
details.   In August, 1940, Neruda was appointed Chilean consul-general in Mexico, where he spent the next three years.
His reputation as a poet had grown steadily during this time,
and his poetry seemed to express the suffering and aspira-
tions of all Latin Americans.   His return to Chile in October,
1943, was a triumphant journey and he found himself acclaimed
by large crowds in country after country.   It was during this
journey that Neruda visited Machu Picchu, which inspired the
poem he composed in Isla Negra two years later.

The year 1945 was very significant in the life of the
poet: he obtained the Premio Nacional de Literatura; he of-
ficially became a member of the Communist Party; he was
elected senator from the provinces of Tarapaca and Antofagasta (northern Chile) with the backing of the working classes;
and he legally changed his name from Ricardo Neftalí Reyes
to Pablo Neruda.   In September of this same year, during a
rest from a period of intense political activities, Neruda
finished "Alturas de Machu Picchu."   He had recently returned
from a tour of the north of Chile, where he had witnessed the
miserable conditions in the nitrate and copper mines.   The po-
verty he found everywhere, and his direct contact with the pro-

letariat, reminded him of his responsibilities as a poet engaged politically since the beginning of the Spanish Civil War.
This preoccupation of putting his art at the service of social
realism, to voice his solidarity with the working people of
Latin America, is once again reflected--as Neruda himself
has admitted--in Section II of the Canto general. [2]

The central symbol of "Alturas de Machu Picchu" is a
journey: the poet's ascent to the ruins of the lost citadel high
up in the Peruvian Andes, where the past seems to come together with the present. This journey is a kind of pilgrimage
through human life in search of meaningful truth. Neruda ex-
plores both his inner world and the past of the American man.
When the poet reaches Machu Picchu, its heights turn out to
be the place from which all existence is explained, including
his own.

The ideology of "Alturas de Machu Picchu" can be explained in terms of Neruda's adherence to a political philosophy
and to the discipline of the Communist Party. In the 12
poems that make up the sequence, we can follow the change
which occurred in Neruda's work: the poet of anguish and
solitude becomes the poet of human solidarity; the metaphysical poetry and the surrealist images of Residencia en la tierra are replaced by the simple exhortation typical of his social
poetry.

"Alturas de Machu Picchu" is perfectly structured and
represents a synthesis of Neruda's earlier works. The first
five poems of the sequence recapitulate images, settings, and
themes which are common to the poetry he composed prior to
"Reunión bajo las nuevas banderas": the interminable flux of
time; isolation and the longing to communicate; earth, wind and
air; sexual love and death; the longing to discern order in life;
the loneliness and the attempt to find a significant identity and
establish a relationship with the rest of mankind. The sixth
poem reveals the name of Machu Picchu for the first time.
The poet has reached the summit and can see and understand
the world beneath him. The last six poems move from the
abstract to the concrete: we have a description of Machu Picchu, and an evocation of the aborigines who built the city of
stone, and of America, buried under the ruins. Section II ends
with an exhortation. The militant poet calls his American
brothers to join him. In their past, and in the future ahead,
he has found the meaningful truth he was seeking.

The social and political themes in "Alturas de Machu

Picchu" are expressed explicitly in the last three poems of
the sequence, as we shall see. Neruda's journey begins with
a profusion of surrealistic images which do not state but suggest:

> From air to air, like an empty net,
> I walked through streets and vapor, arriving
>   and sending forth
> in the coming of autumn the offered coins
>   of leaves,
> and, between the spring and ears of wheat,
> that which the greatest love, as though
>   caught within a fallen glove,
> gives us like a stretched moon.
>
> (Days of live radiance in the inclemency
> of bodies: weapons converted
> to the silence of acid:
> nights frayed down to the last flour:
> assaulted stamens of the nuptial land.)
>
> Someone who awaited me amid the violins
> found a world like a buried tower
> sinking its spiral deeper than all
> the harsh sulphur-colored leaves:
> and deeper yet, in a layer of gold,
> like a sword swathed in meteors,
> I sank a turbulent and tender hand
> to the most visceral parts of the earth.
>
> I placed my forehead amid deep waves,
> I descended, like a drop, into sulphuric peace,
> and, like a blind man, I returned to the jasmine
> of our spent human spring. [3]
>
> Del aire al aire, como una red vacía,
> iba yo entre las calles y la atmósfera,
>   llegando y despidiendo,
> en el advenimiento del otoño la moneda extendida
> de las hojas, y entre la primavera y las espigas,
> lo que el más grande amor, como dentro de
>   un guante
> que cae, nos entrega como una larga luna.
>
> (Días de fulgor vivo en la intemperie
> de los cuerpos: aceros convertidos
> al silencio del ácido:

noches deshilachadas hasta la última harina:
estambres agredidos de la patria nupcial.)

Alguien que me esperó entre los violines
encontró un mundo como una torre enterrada
hundiendo su espiral más abajo de todas
las hojas de color de ronco azufre:
más abajo, en el oro de la geología,
como una espada envuelta en meteoros,
hundí la mano turbulenta y dulce
en lo más genital de lo terrestre.

Puse la frente entre las olas profundas,
descendí como una gota entre la paz sulfúrica,
y, como un ciego, regresé al jazmín
de la gastada primavera humana [OC 312]. ³

This opening section shows us Neruda seeking inward and
downward for a concealed "vein of gold," then sinking lower
still in the more "visceral" depths of the earth in a blind
search to rediscover our "exhausted human springs."⁴ Although there are many indefinite allusions in the poem--"del
aire al aire," or "alguien que me esperó entre los violines"--
to which a precise meaning cannot be affixed, the idea of a
journey is conveyed clearly by the verbal forms "iba," "descendí," "regresé." Following the poet's itinerary in the
next four poems, we shall see that he comes face to face with
death before he is able to gain knowledge of the meaning of
life.

The second fragment of "Alturas de Machu Picchu"
contrasts the order found in nature with the disorder found in
man:

Flower to flower surrenders its seed
and rock maintains its scattered flower
in a battered dress of diamond and sand,
man crumples the petals of the light he gathers
in the fixed origins of the sea,
and pierces the palpitating metal in his hands.
And soon, between clothes and smoke, upon the
          sunken table,
the soul remains like a shuffled deck ...

Si la flor a la flor entrega el alto germen
y la roca mantiene su flor diseminada
en su golpeado traje de diamante y arena,

> el hombre arruga el pétalo de la luz que recoge
> en los determinados manantiales marinos
> y talandra el metal palpitante en sus manos.
> Y pronto, entre la ropa y el humo, sobre la
>   mesa hundida,
> como una barajada cantidad queda el alma ...
> [OC 313].

Nature is self-perpetuating, rich and fecund in its cycles, sprouting on fertile soil and even in the rocks. Man, on the other hand, loses his freedom to the world of objects until he becomes aware that his own soul is left impoverished.

The poet longs for truth, the kind of truth he had once perceived in a stone. But he cannot find it in the urban centers he has left behind, where he sees the empty faces of men who like robots go to their factories, their department stores, their mechanized tasks. He asks:

> What was man? In what part of his empty talk
> among his shops and sirens, in which of his
>   metallic movements
> lived the indestructible, the undying, life?

> Qué era el hombre? En que parte de su
>   conversación abierta
> entre los almacenes y los silbidos, en cual de
>   sus movimientos metálicos
> vivía lo indestructible, lo imperecedero,
>   la vida? [OC 314].

The answer to this question does not appear in the three subsequent poems, which deal with two facets of death: one, great and noble like the essence of life, which cannot be found in the cities; the other, less impressive and miserable, which hovers in congested metropolitan centers.

The latter is the subject of the third poem. In this fragment Neruda looks at modern man's withering existence: seeing it gradually husked off the cob like maize, in a humiliating process, and not proudly scythed away with a single stroke. Neruda looks at man's life as a wasting death "in a black cup. " The image of the black cup--as Robert Pring-Mill has pointed out--"prepares the way for the contrasting image of Machu Picchu as a 'permanence of stone ... raised like a chalice'. "5

In the fourth poem, Neruda uses sea imagery to depict a more noble death: as the tide is at the ebb, reaching its lowest point, so man's existence fades away. This inevitable death is the same Neruda portrays in the poems of Residencia en la tierra. What is disconcerting is not man's doubt about the afterlife, but the belief that death is the total negation of man's existence. The theme of love for one's fellow men is also introduced in this fragment, but the love remains unrealizable as long as all the poet sees of them is their daily deaths.

Neruda visualizes his own insignificant death in an empty mood, which recalls the anguish of his earlier work:

I went, then, street by street, river by river,
city by city, bed by bed,
my salt mask passing through a desert,
till in the last miserable houses, without lamp,
        without fire,
without bread or stone or silence, alone,
I rolled, dying of my own death.

Entonces fui por calle y calle y río y río,
y ciudad y ciudad y cama y cama,
y atrovesó el desierto mi máscara salobre
y en las últimas casas humilladas, sin lámparas,
        sin fuego,
sin pan, sin piedra, sin silencio, sólo,
rodé muriendo de mi propia muerte [OC 315].

The last verse announces a very definite and degrading death. This is reflected in the reiteration of the concept of dying, the alliteration, and the use of the verb "rodar, " "to roll, " more adequate in expressing the motion of an object than that of a person.

Using a series of surrealistic images, Neruda defines death in the short fifth poem of the sequence:

It was not you, solemn death, bird of iron plumage
that the poor inheritor of such dwellings
carried among his hasty rations, under vacuous skin:
it was, instead, a pitiful strand of old rope:
inner strength which did not come forth,
harsh dew that didn't turn to sweat.
That which could not be reborn, a particle
of insignificant death, without peace or grave:
a bone or a bell that died from within.

I lifted the bandages of iodine and sank my hands
in the feeble pains that killed death
and found nothing in the wound save a cold gust
        of wind
that entered and chilled the nebulous crevices
        of my soul.

No eras tú, muerte grave, ave de plumas férreas,
la que el pobre heredero de las habitaciones
llevaba entre alimentos apresurados, bajo
        la piel vacía:
era algo, un pobre pétalo de cuerda exterminada:
un átomo del pecho que no vino al combate
o el áspero rocío que no cayó en la frente.
Era lo que no pudo renacer, un pedazo
de la pequeña muerte sin paz ni territorio:
un hueso, una campana que morían en él.

Yo levanté las vendas del yodo, hundí las manos
en los pobres dolores que mataban la muerte,
y no encontré en la herida sino una racha fría
que entraba en los vagos intersticios del alma
        [OC 316].

Its conclusion refers to modern life, described in the last two
verses with nothing in its wounds except cold gusts of wind
that chill one's soul. We have reached the lowest point of the
entire sequence. After the poet has identified himself with his
past, and with the sufferings of the American man, he is
ready to ascend to the heights of Machu Picchu.

    Just as "Reunión bajo las nuevas banderas" represents
a break in Neruda's poetic evolution, incorporating his earlier
work and presenting it from a social perspective, so fragment
six of "Alturas de Machu Picchu" represents a break within
the poem, embodying the content of the preceding fragments
and preparing the way for Neruda's social and political message.

    As Neruda climbs upward in space toward the heights,
the poem itself seems to rise:

Then up the ladder made of earth I climbed
through vast undergrowth of lost jungle
until I touched you, Machu Picchu.

High city of stepped stone,

a dwelling at last
not hidden in mundane sleeping garments.
In you, like two parallel lines,
the cradle of lightning and of man
rocked in a wind of thorns.

Mother of stone, sperm of condor.

High reef of human dawn.

Spade lost in primordial sand.

Entonces en la escala de la tierra he subido
entre la atroz maraña de las selvas perdidas
hasta ti, Machu Picchu.

Alta ciudad de piedras escalares,
por fin morada del que lo terrestre
no escondió en las dormidas vestiduras.
En ti, como dos líneas paralelas,
la cuna del relámpago y del hombre
se mecían en un viento de espinas.

Madre de piedra, espuma de los cóndores.

Alto arrecife de la aurora humana.

Pala perdida en la primera arena [OC 316].

As he reaches the summit, he looks back in time towards the
moment when the city was erected. Suddenly past and present
seem to make sense--a sense which later on will turn out to
be the reunification of the Inca world with contemporary American man. The two parallel lines that meet symbolize the
death of insignificant men and the permanence of the citadel.
Machu Picchu brings back to life an ancient kingdom, with its
triangular structures and simple architecture. This is the
location where the "maize grew high," and where the vicuña
fleece was woven. But all that was transitory has disappeared
and what endures is the city of stone collectively built by the
men of the past.

The contrast between what endures and what has van-
ished is emphasized in the seventh poem. The death of the
men who built Machu Picchu is depicted as being nobler because it was a collective experience. What these men left behind was a city "raised like a chalice in all those hands,"

whose permanence is symbolized by the image of an "ever-lasting rose. "

Neruda sees in the death of these men a built-in les-son for the future, and he identifies himself with them. His search for noble death has also been the search for a more significant existence in their company. The poet's journey upward in space and backward in time does not end with the discovery of Machu Picchu living its enduring "life of stone. " For the next two poems, Neruda exalts the city with powerful lyricism.

The eighth poem takes us a step further in the past. It is a vivid evocation of pre-Columbian man and of nature. Neruda summons his American ancestor with a call of love:

> Arise with me, American love.
>
> Kiss with me the secret stones.
>
> . . .
>
> Come to my very being, to my own dawn.
>
> Sube conmigo, amor americano.
>
> Besa conmigo las piedras secretas.
>
> . . .
>
> Ven a mi propio ser, al alba mía [OC 318, 320f].

In these verses there is already an indication of the more personal summons to his past brothers, which we find in poem XI.

The ninth poem of the sequence is a solemn chant to Machu Picchu, written mostly in hendecasyllables and de-scribing the site with 84 epithets. Not one single verb ap-pears in this fragment, which is composed in the style of a liturgical litany, with an abundance of repetitive phrases:

> Triangular tunic, pollen of stone.
>
> Lamp of granite, bread of stone.
>
> Mineral serpent, rose of stone.
>
> Buried ship, source of stone.
>
> Horse of the moon, light of stone.
>
> Equinoctial quadrant, vapor of stone.

Final geometry, book of stone.

Túnica triangular, polen de piedra.

Lámpara de granito, pan de piedra.

Serpiente mineral, rosa de piedra.

Nave enterrada, manantial de piedra.

Caballo de la luna, luz de piedra.

Escuadra equinoccial, vapor de piedra.

Geometría final, libro de piedra [OC 320].

The entire poem is a "crescendo" culminating in the last two lines, which orient our thoughts towards the multitude of men who carried gigantic stones to build the city.

The last major turning point of "Alturas de Machu Picchu" comes in the tenth fragment. We are dealing here with a social poetry that has a clear political aim. The poet once again turns to man, the true subject of this section of the Canto general. He compares the men of the past with those of the present, and wonders whether the Incas, responsible for the grandeur of Machu Picchu, may not perhaps have been like urban men today, erecting the city on a base of human suffering. He asks:

Stone within stone, and man, where was he?
Air within air, and man, where was he?
Time within time, and man, where was he?

Piedra en la piedra, el hombre, dónde estuvo?
Aire en el aire, el hombre, dónde estuvo?
Tiempo en el tiempo, el hombre, dónde estuvo?
[OC 321].

If slaves built the city with stone upon stone, in what conditions did they live? Were starvation and human exploitation as common in ancient America as in modern America?

In the last two fragments, Neruda abandons his passive attitude which had characterized poems I to X. He rises before the ruins and demands that the dead slaves be returned to him. He becomes the active poet who wants to rescue the humble man, whose name, Juan, is the same as that of the earth ("La tierra se llama Juan," Section VIII of the Canto general). This Juan is a worker who descends from Viracocha,

the legendary Father of the Incas. The association of a Spanish name with an Indian name symbolizes the union of the two
races, who had been enemies before. The product of these
two races is the American man.

In the last poem of the sequence Neruda wants to be
the spokesman of all men who died building Machu Picchu, so
that they may rise again to birth, as his brothers. He wants
to be the link between past and present so that he can build a
better future for America. "Sube a nacer conmigo, hermano"
is the call of the militant poet who wants to identify himself
with the workers:

> Farmer, weaver, silent shepherd,
> tamer of tutelar guanacos:
> mason of the daring scaffold:
> bearer of Andean tears:
> jeweler with crushed fingers:
> tiller trembling among seeds:
> potter amid spilled clay:
> bring to the cup of this new life
> your ancient, buried sorrows
> . . .
> sharpen the knives you put away . . .

> Labrador, tejedor, pastor callado:
> domador de guanacos tutelares:
> albañil del andamio desafiado:
> aguador de las lágrimas andinas:
> joyero de los dedos machacados:
> agricultor temblando en la semilla:
> alfarero en tu greda derramado:
> traed a la copa de esta nueva vida
> vuestros viejos dolores enterrados.
> . . .
> afilad los cuchillos que guardasteis . . . [OC 324].

The call to violence in the last verse cited, and the
concluding exhortation of the poem, clearly show the political
aim of "Alturas de Machu Picchu." The poet abandons the
initial pessimism and becomes involved in a social struggle for
justice:

> Give me silence, water, hope.

> Give me struggle, iron, volcanoes.

> Let bodies press against me like magnets.

Come swiftly to my veins and to my mouth.

Speak through my words and through my blood.

Dadme el silencio, el agua, la esperanza.

Dadme la lucha, el hierro, los volcanes.

Apegadme los cuerpos como imanes.

Acudid a mis venas y a mi boca.

Hablad por mis palabras y mi sangre [OC 324].

Thus ends Section II of the Canto general. In the space of 12 short fragments we have followed Neruda's journey, which has symbolically linked him to the American man in a fraternal bond.

Conclusion to Part I

In the social and political themes of Neruda's poetry from 1936 to 1950, we can detect a personal concern for humanity that was absent in his earlier work. From "Reunión bajo las nuevas banderas" to Canto general, one important change underlies Neruda's poetic evolution: his social themes acquire a political character. The negative vision of the world, the rainy and solitary depiction of the south of Chile, the preoccupation with death, and the anguish caused by frustrated love and by the inability to communicate, which were the predominant themes of the poems written prior to the Spanish Civil War, are replaced now with a social poetry which sings of universal love and with a political position which finds hope in the future.

There is at times a forced prosaic tone in some of the poems of the Canto general, as we have seen. When this occurs, the poet's lyricism suffers because it is disrupted by violence or by diatribes. We must keep in mind, however, that books such as España en el corazón or the Canto general were written during times of political and ideological crisis, and that the political propaganda within them was not excessive.

The step from a desperate pessimism to the optimism of certain poems, such as "América, no invoco tu nombre en vano," reflects a change in the poet's attitude. After his political conversion, Neruda fights his personal desolation and sees hope in the fate of mankind. His political activism and his pledge to attain social justice restore his faith in life.

In most of the poetry of this period, Neruda expresses himself as a writer in solidarity with the people. In this respect, his work is common to that of other Hispanic writers. Federico de Onís has affirmed that the "dehumanization of art" is impossible in Latin America since poets feel united to present-day problems, to their land and their people. Hence, it is not surprising that their work may reflect social and political ideas.[1] This is the case of Pablo Neruda. His attitude of protest is the same as that of other writers, such as Rafael Alberti or César Vallejo, who have denounced social and political conditions in their countries and in the world.

The change of orientation in Neruda's work is the product of two major events in his life: his witnessing of the
Spanish Civil War and his adherence to the Communist Party.
As a result, he becomes the poet who seeks what his own experience has in common with the experience of other men;
the poet who has a need to show men to themselves in such a
way that they can feel the identity behind their separate lives,
and share his insights--as he does in "Alturas de Machu Picchu"; and the poet who, because of his political beliefs, becomes the spokesman of the deprived and sings of their hope.

In Las uvas y el viento, written in 1954, Neruda's social and political doctrine is reiterated:

> I believe
> that we will not join together
> in the heights.
> I believe
> that beneath the earth nothing awaits us,
> but above the ground
> we go together.
> Our unity is above the earth.

> Creo
> que no nos juntaremos
> en la altura.
> Creo
> que bajo de la tierra nada nos espera,
> pero sobre la tierra
> vamos juntos.
> Nuestra unidad está sobre la tierra [OC 683].

These verses summarize the social and political themes which
were predominant in his poetry from 1936 to 1950.

There are two main periods in the poetry of Pablo Neruda, as we have seen. There is the lyrical assertion of the
natural world and of the individual human being as part of it,
reflected in the earlier poems. And there is the social participation of the poet who identifies himself with his fellow
men, as well as an austere vision of the seer who knows that
the world is full of tragedy and injustice, reflected in the
"engaged poetry." The first period is characterized by pessimism, the second by optimism. The poem that marks the
division between these two periods is "Reunión bajo las nuevas banderas."

With España en el corazón and with the last section of Tercera residencia, Neruda gives us a poetry whose foundations rest on the doctrine of social realism. The Canto general is a lyrical attempt on the part of the poet to interpret the destiny of America from both the historical and political perspectives. In the analysis constituting Part I, I have concentrated on the political poetry because no other critic has ever treated it as a whole. I have also tried to give an understanding of Neruda through a specific aspect of his poetry. In Part II, the process shall be reversed in an attempt to understand the Obras as a whole through a specific aspect of the poet, himself. Consequently, there shall be more biographical information and less critical analysis of individual poems.

Facing page: Delia del Carril (left) and Pablo Neruda, ca. 1947, visit Chilean fellow poet Gabriela Mistral, winner of 1945 Nobel Prize for Literature. (Courtesy of Emilio Ellena and the Departamento de Fotografía y Microfilm, Universidad de Chile.)

Drawing of Neruda by Bono (Anita Bernard), 1977.

Facing page: A document signed boldly in blue by "Neruda"
stating his artistic credo in especially visual terms (shown
here at 65 per cent of true size). (Courtesy Emilio Ellena.)
A translation by Salvatore Bizzarro appears beneath it.

Los preclaros lineales grabaron en Altamira los límites entre la bestia y la inteligencia y hasta ahora nuestros antepasados roquerizos trazaron la frontera que persiste.

La línea es la severidad de la música y la extensión de la mano y del pensamiento.

Yo soy poeta lineal, es decir, justiciero, testimonial de cuanto existe, porque sin mano dirigida y sin línea directora, no existe mundo. El mundo es una línea.

Es un honor para mi poesía abrir la puerta del espacio de Chile para que los que graban diseñen el universo que nos pertenece porque lo conquistaremos: a fuerza de línea, es decir de eternidad.

Prehistoric artists engraved in Altamira rock the lines dividing bestiality and intelligence--and all our ancestors since the stoneage have retraced this persisting frontier. / The line is the rigor of music, the extension of the hand and of thought. / I am a poet of line--that is, just, a witness to all that exists, for without the guided hand and without the directing line, the world does not exist. The world is a line. / It is an honor for my poetry to open the door onto Chile so that those who engrave lines may delineate the whole universe--it belongs to us because we shall conquer it: with the force of line, that is, eternity.

Part II

V

EVOLUTION TOWARD A SIMPLER FORM

The publication in 1954 of the Odas elementales, followed almost immediately by the Nuevas odas elementales a
year later, and the Tercer libro de las odas, in 1957, reveal
a new aspect in Neruda's poetry: the search for simplicity
and the aspiration of transforming a poem into a useful object of art. The poet becomes infatuated with facticity, he is
attentive of the smallest detail, and he discovers and inter-
prets the unsuspecting and hidden poetry of the small things
that surround us, that go almost unnoticed, and that he loves.
His Odes are a song to matter, and even things that could
be considered vulgar are resplendent in his verses: the savo-
ry artichoke; the onion, destined to glow on the table of the
poor as a "spherical water rose"; the tomato, which is also
delectable to the eyes; the fallen chestnut, whose seed will
bring forth a new tree; the wild flowers that grow in the
fields; the Chilean birds; and the murmuring sea. There are
odes to oil, to the stars, the ocean, liver, to man's most
humble possessions, such as socks, soap, bread; odes to the
hands, to the smell of wood, to the bees, the albatross, the
algae, the tuna in the market place, splendid still life colored
like a painting; odes to the abandoned house, the spoon, the
color green, the butterfly, the lemon, the magnolia and the
apple; and there are odes to poetry, and to the master poets
Jorge Manrique, Rimbaud and Walt Whitman. The list is not
complete. But in the three books of Odes the poet sings the
essential themes of mankind: the elements that make up the
material world, either in their pure form (air, fire, sea) or
in their concrete and individual form (salt, wine, seagull).
He will turn to nature and to a nostalgic remembrance of the
Chilean landscape; he perceives his youth in the smell of
wood; in the funereal algae he sees the coast; and he is saddened by the constant rain. Together with elemental things,
Neruda will sing his elemental experiences. Even the odes
that carry a political or social message, such as the "Ode to

a Butterfly, " the "Ode to Sadness, " the "Ode to a Nocturnal Washerwoman, " the "Ode to a Dead Millionaire, " do not correspond to a set political formula as did his social and political poetry examined in previous chapters. We are faced with a poet who has put aside his revolutionary hymns and is willing to share with us all his knowledge and perceptions of everyday life. Most of this poetry is joyful, optimistic, and clear as crystal, even though, at times, it is tainted with an occasional tear. For example, the "Ode to the Algae of the Ocean" reminds us of the gloomy sorrow of Residencia en la tierra. But the sadness alternates with happiness, and most of the things we see are permeated with serenity and a bucolic peace.

Prior to the Odes, Neruda had tried in vain to resolve one of the most bothersome conflicts within his writings: how to represent the "ordinary people" and yet at the same time write in a style comprehensible to them. Furthermore, he found no answer to certain questions he posed for himself again and again: how could his art relate to the practical, sober, normal actuality of life? And how could beauty react to the demands of the so-called "normal existence, " on which society appeared to rest, and upon which it appeared to build? Either he would have to purify his poetry of all hermeticism and decadence or renounce his call as the poet of the people.

Beginning with the Odas elementales, Neruda is caught in the struggle between his artistic aspiration and his need to reach the masses, in an attempt to combine somehow these conflicting opposites and to reconcile them. From this point it becomes the story of the artist who is painfully aware of the gulf between his artistic temperament and the apparent, healthy, solid world of the simple folk. The poet does not resign himself to either of the two extremes. In the end, he realizes that it is his love and compassion for the ordinary people and their humaneness which is for him the main source of all that is of value in his art. After years of inner strife, the poet succeeds in overcoming the conflict in the reconciliation of the concrete (life) with the abstract (art). By giving evidence of his confirmation of a positive existence, of a striving toward the preservation and the rehabilitation of humanity, Neruda has distanced himself from the hopelessness of his two Residencias and the anger of España en el corazón. The Odes constitute a new period in his writings, as he attempts to capture the essential in the particular through an understanding of the intrinsic wonders of reality.

It is inevitable that Neruda's search for simplicity leads at times to prosaic verses, as we find, for example, in the "Ode to Criticism," where he warns his critics to leave his poetry to the common folks, for whom it is intended; and that not all the new poetry is valid from an artistic point of view.   There are some odes that deal mainly with personal and polemical leitmotifs or sing political themes which fall short of his lyrical potential (excluding, of course, the "Ode to Guatemala," a transparent hymn to the Central American nation).   These odes are still interesting, but show us a writer we already know: the committed poet who fulfills his proletarian duty as a social realist.   We are more concerned with the intimate Neruda, who finds poetry in an insect, a dead tree, or a pair of socks, and who can be understood by almost anyone.

Paradoxically, this is a man who has adopted a commonplace view of reality, and has become dependent on the language of the ordinary man.   He has abandoned his disregard for syntax and grammar, and he no longer uses the verbal instrument at his disposal to create those long, difficult, spirited verses devoid of logic and full of bizarre imagery. His word order now flows simply and rhythmically, as we can clearly see in his "Ode to the Dictionary," and in many other odes.   He is a poet who wants to sing a coherent world, rational and structured, and he is now ready to tell us in the "Ode to a Seagull": "I am a realist poet/ photographer of the sky" ("Soy poeta realista/ fotógrafo del cielo").

In the "Ode to Poetry" Neruda manifests his poetic creed:

> I asked you to be
> utilitarian and useful
> like metal or flour,
> willing to be plow,
> tool,
> bread and wine,
> willing, oh Poetry,
> to fight in a hand to hand combat
> and to fall bleeding to death.
>
> Yo te pedí que fueras
> utilitaria y útil
> como metal o harina,
> dispuesta a ser arado,
> herramienta,

> pan y vino,
> dispuesta, poesía,
> a luchar cuerpo a cuerpo
> y a caer desangrándote [OC 1076-7].

And in the "House of the Odes," which heads the collection
<u>Nuevas odas elementales</u> and reitirates his poetic manifesto,
Neruda declares:

> I want everything
> to have
> a handle,
> everything to be
> cup or tool.
>
> Quiero que todo
> tenga
> empuñadura,
> que todo sea
> taza o herramienta [OC 1130].

By saying "I want everything to be cup or tool," Neruda
is interested in transforming his poetry into a useful object.
And by giving his verses a "handle," the poet removes them
from the exclusive realm of art.   It would be a mistake,
though, to think that Neruda, in order to reach the masses,
has lowered the quality of his poetry.   As it would to assume
that the masses did not understand his writings simply because they did not understand some of his imagery.

Perhaps Fernando Alegría is the critic who has understood best why Neruda has chosen this particular style and this
particular verse in the <u>Odes</u>:

> Neruda uses a peculiarly short, irregular line, not
> out of mere whimsy but because he believes this
> type of line performs a definite functional purpose.
> It would be a great mistake, therefore, to attempt
> to put these <u>Odes</u> in prose form, as someone has
> suggested, or to change in any way the order of the
> lines.   Just as the aesthetic object here is a com-
> pendium of the poet's entire concept of the world,
> so the short line is in itself a definition. . . .   In its
> aerial structure, the Nerudian <u>Ode</u> is like a tall
> building made of glass and steel to support an in-
> visible but formidable mass.   The <u>Odes</u>' lightness
> and plasticity guarantee their strength.   In this poet-

ic architecture every corner line becomes a live
and resplendent fire of images which give birth to
other images and still others, until the small edi-
fice seems to burn in its entirety with inextinguish-
able vigor: it is an elemental fire fed by the com-
bustion of the essential components of man's life. [1]

In the three books of Odes, many are the poems that
show us the intimate Neruda. Because they reach a high level
of lyricism even in translation my preferences are: "Ode to
an Onion, " "Ode to Salt, " "Ode to a Blue Flower, " "Ode to a
Pair of Socks, " "Ode to Walt Whitman, " "Ode to the Wandering Albatross, " "Ode to a Dead Carob Tree, " and "Ode to a
Star. " The themes of these odes are varied, as we can see
even from the excerpts offered here. What they have in common is their human and universal content. They speak for
themselves and for everyone. For the poet, the present and
the past are keenly and personally felt in their living warmth
or in their extensive pain, but they are always felt in the context of his human experience.

In the "Ode to an Onion, " for example, Neruda calls
it "star of the poor, " destined to "stave off the hunger of the
laborer along his toilsome way. " The poem is topical. But
it is not a good poem because of it. Rather, the reverse is
true. It is a good poem because the poet puts what is topical
into a perspective which surprises us because it shows us that
in front of our eyes there was always much more than what
we saw:

> Onion,
> luminous flask,
> petal by petal
> was your beauty formed,
> crystalline flakes made you grow
> and, in the dark secret of earth,
> your girth swelled up with dewdrops.

> Cebolla,
> luminosa redoma,
> pétalo a pétalo
> se formó tu hermosura,
> escamas de cristal te acrecentaron
> y en el secreto de la tierra oscura
> se redondeó tu vientre de rocío [OC 964].

In the "Ode to Salt, " Neruda talks of the mineral in

the mines and in the sea, calling it "mountain of buried
light/ transparent cathedral/ crystal of the sea/ oblivion of
the waves." He tells us that salt gives us the "central fla-
vor of the infinite" either in the "saline pampas" or in the
"trails of foam" of the ocean. But while the salt in the
mines sings a "pitiful song" as it is extracted from the bow-
els of the earth, the sea salt, full of goodness, spreads an
essential light upon food:

> Sea dust, the tongue
> is kissed by you ...
> ...
> taste fuses in each
> seasoned morsel your oceanity ...
>
> Polve del mar, la lengua
> de ti recibe un beso ...
> ...
> el gusto funde en cada
> sazonado manjar tu oceanía ... [OC 1430].

Salt, with light and fire, is one of the elements responsible for the purity of a flower the poet finds during a
walk by the ocean in "Ode to a Blue Flower:"

> By the sea, walking,
> in the month of November,
> amid the shrubs that receive
> light, fire, and marine salt,
> I found a blue flower
> born in the harshest meadowlands.
> ...
> I took it in my hands
> and I admired it as if the sea lived
> in only one drop,
> or as if in the strife
> of land and sea
> a flower would raise
> a small emblem
> of blue fire, of irresistible peace,
> of untamed genuineness.
>
> Cerca del mar, andando,
> en el mes de noviembre,
> entre los matorrales que reciben
> luz, fuego y sal marinas,
> hallé una flor azul

nacida en la durísima pradera.
...
La levanté en mis manos
y la miré como si el mar viviera
en una sola gota,
como si en el combate
de la tierra y las aguas
una flor levantara
un pequeño estandarte
de fuego azul, de paz irresistible,
de indómita pureza ⌈OC 994⌉.

In this blue flower, mysterious product of land and water,
Neruda finds the triumph of "irresistible peace."

        Like many other odes in the collection, the "Ode to a
Pair of Socks" ends with a moral.   But it is by no means a
sermon.   It is a simple and gentle story full of philosophical
wisdom.   Fernando Alegría calls it a "lyrical pastime"[2]:

Maru Mori brought me
a pair
of socks
she weaved with her hands
of shepherd
...
Violent socks,
my feet became
two woolen fish,
two long sharks
of ultramarine blue
pierced
by a golden tress
...
Thus
my feet
were honored
by
these
celestial
socks.
...
Nevertheless,
I resisted
the strong temptation
to save them
as school boys

preserve
fireflies,
as academicians
collect
rare documents
. . .
I stretched out my feet
and covered them
with
the beautiful
socks
. . .
And this is
the moral of my ode:
beauty
is beauty twice
and what is good is doubly
good
when it concerns two woolen
socks
in winter.

Me trajo Maru Mori
un par
de calcetines
que tejió con sus manos
de pastora
. . .
Violentos calcetines
mis pies fueron
dos pescados
de lana,
dos largos tiburones
de azul ultramarino
atravesados
por una trenza de oro
. . .
mis pies
fueron honrados
de este modo
por
estos
celestiales
calcetines
. . .
Sin embargo
resistí

la tentación aguda
de guardarlos
como los colegiales
preservan
las luciérnagas,
como los eruditos
coleccionan
documentos sagrados
. . .
estiré
los pies
y me enfundé
los bellos
calcetines
. . .
Y es esta
la moral de mi oda:
dos veces es belleza
la belleza
y lo que es bueno es doblemente
bueno
cuando se trata de dos calcetines
de lana
en el invierno [OC 1149f, 1151].

In the "Ode to Walt Whitman," Neruda celebrates the great North American bard who had been his inspiration since an early age.   Whitman had sung the American people and the American landscape, his love for elemental things, and his faith in his own elemental experiences.   Now, a hundred years after his death, he symbolically guides the South American by the hand:

I do not remember
at what age,
or where,
whether in the great wet South
or on the dreadful
coast, beneath the brief
shriek of the seagull,
I touched a hand and it was
the hand of Walt Whitman:
I trampled the earth
with bare feet,
and I walked upon the grass,
on the enduring dew
of Walt Whitman.

Yo no recuerdo
a qué edad,
ni dónde,
si en el gran Sur mojado
on en la costa
temible, bajo el breve
grito de las gaviotas,
toqué una mano y era
la mano de Walt Whitman:
pisé la tierra
con los pies desnudos
anduve sobre el pasto,
sobre el firme rocío
de Walt Whitman [OC 1275].

Neruda calls Whitman "first cousin" and tells him that
since his death new and cruel things have come to pass: those
who have assassinated Lincoln "now lie in his bed. " Unfortu-
nately, before dying they "raised a throne/ spattered/ by mis-
fortune and blood. " In spite of all this, Walt Whitman's voice
is still heard, and his people do not forget him.   They still
gather singing beneath the magnitude of his "spacious life, "
and walk "caressing/ the pure development/ of fraternity on
earth. "

In Walt Whitman, Neruda sees a poetic projection of
himself, and what the former says about himself can also ap-
ply to the latter:

I celebrate myself, and sing myself,
And what I assume you shall assume,
For every atom belonging to me as good
        belongs to you. [3]

Like the North American, he, too, wants to be the poet of
collective experiences and the "vox populi. "

The next two odes, the "Ode to the Wandering Albatross" and the "Ode to a Dead Carob Tree, " show us a melancholy Neruda preoccupied with an acute sense of solitude--not-
withstanding the overall message of hope expressed in the
three books of Odes.

In the "Ode to the Wandering Albatross, " the poet
wants to determine the cause that made the huge bird leave his
homeland in New Zealand and cross the ocean to Chile, where
he dies on the damp sands of autumn.   But he concludes that
no one can ever know:

Why? Why? What salt,
what wave, what wind
did it search in the sea?
What gave it strength
against the immensity
of space?
Why was its endurance
tested in the most desolate
solitudes?
Or was its destination
the magnetic rose
of a star?
No one
can know the answer, or tell it.

¿Por qué? ¿Por qué? ¿Qué sal,
qué ola, qué viento
busco en el mar?
¿Qué levantó su fuerza
contra todo
el espacio?
¿Por qué su poderío
se probó en las más duras
soledades?
¿O fue su meta
la magnética rosa
de una estrella?
Nadie podrá saberlo, ni decirlo
        [OC 1294].

For Neruda, the bird's crossing was a singular feat, but no
one shall pay tribute to this hero of other lands who, at the
completion of its lonely voyage, met death on the Chilean
shore. The only thing the poet can do is write these verses
"in memoriam. "

        The theme of a solitary death is repeated in the "Ode
to a Dead Carob Tree. " Neruda mourns what only the day
before was a robust tree casting a majestic shade upon the
plain. But the American storm came to the carob tree and
"with a bolt from heaven/ toppled its beauty. "

        It was hard and furrowed
        by time, a solid
        column wrought
        by rain and earth,
        and like a candelabrum distributed

its spherical
wooden arms
whence it squandered
green light and green shade
upon the meadow.

Era duro y arado
por el tiempo, una firme
columna trabajada
por la lluvia y la tierra
y como un candelabro repartía
sus redondeados
brazos de madera
desde donde
luz verde y sombra verde
prodigó a la llanura [OC 1298].

Neruda calls the tree his "dead brother," but cannot weep and
takes his leave, leaving only the wind to look after him.

"Ode to a Star" is a fantasy about light. Using surrealistic imagery and a simple language the poet recounts his
encounter with the celestial body:

Reaching out at the night
on the terrace
of a very tall and sullen skyscraper,
I could touch the nocturnal canopy
and in an act of extraordinary love
I grabbed a celestial star.

The night was dark,
and I sneaked away
along the street
with a stolen star in my pocket.

It looked like
trembling crystal,
and suddenly
it was
as if I were carrying
a package of ice
or an archangel's sword in my belt.

Fearful,
I kept it
under my bed,
to prevent anyone from finding it,
but its light

pierced
at first
the woolen mattress,
then
the shingles,
and the roof of my house.

Troublesome
became for me
my most private needs.

Always with that light
of astral acetylene
that throbbed as if wanting
to return to the night,
I could not bother with all
my chores
and thus it was that I forgot to pay
        my bills
and found myself without bread or
        provisions.

Meanwhile, in the streets,
the passersby mutinied, mundane
sellers
attracted, no doubt,
by the unusual brightness
they saw pouring out my window.

Then,
I picked up
my star again,
with care
I wrapped it in my handkerchief
and masked, through the crowd,
I slipped unnoticed.

I headed west,
to the point of the Río Verde
which lies serene
beneath the willows.

I took the star of the cold night
and gently
threw it in the waters.

And I was not surprised
that it drew away
like an insoluble fish
agitating
in the night of the river
its diamantine body.

Asomado a la noche
en la terraza
de un rascacielos altísimo y amargo
pude tocar la bóveda nocturna
y en un acto de amor extraordinario
me apoderé de una celeste estrella.

Negra estaba la noche
y yo me deslizaba
por la calle
con la estrella robada en el bolsillo.
De cristal tembloroso
parecía
y era
de pronto
como si llevara
un paquete de hielo
o una espada de arcángel en el cinto.

La guardé
temoroso
debajo de la cama
para que no la descubriera nadie,
pero su luz
atravesó
primero
la lana del colchón,
luego
las tejas,
el techo de mi casa.

Incómodos
se hicieron
para mí
los más privados menesteres.

Siempre con esa luz
de astral acetileno
que palpitaba como si quisiera
regresar a la noche,
yo no podía
preocuparme de todos
mis deberes
y así fue que olvidé pagar mis cuentas
y me quedé sin pan ni provisiones.

Mientras tanto, en la calle,
se amotinaban
transeúntes, mundanos
vendedores

atraídos sin duda
por el fulgor insólito
que veían salir de mi ventana.

Entonces
recogí
otra vez mi estrella,
con cuidado
la envolví en mi pañuelo
y enmascarado entre la muchedumbre
pude pasar sin ser reconocido.

Me dirigí al oeste,
al Río Verde,
que allí bajo los sauces
es sereno.

Tomé la estrella de la noche fría
y suavemente
la eché sobre las aguas.

Y no me sorprendió
que se alejara
como un pez insoluble
moviendo
en la noche del río
su cuerpo de diamante [OC 1367-9].

In these books of Odes, as in most of his poetry, Neruda is indebted to nature for his more direct, sensuous, and nonintellectual modes of perception.   "Ode to a Star" is a good example of this.   Other examples are the poems to the birds of America, which exhibit the most lucid particulars of ornithology, and the "Ode to Winter," which offers perhaps the richest imagery of the entire collection.   But it is in the simpler expressions that Neruda finds correspondences to human life, and these become the source of his new poetry.

In two of his best books published after the Odes, Estravagario (1958) and Memorial de Isla Negra (1964), Neruda insists on being what a critic has called "el poeta de la sencillez," "the poet of simplicity."[4]   He does not always succeed, but it would be erroneous to doubt his sincerity.   The poems in both collections are much more personal and are rich in autobiographical details.

In Estravagario, brilliantly translated into English by Alastair Reid,[5] the poet celebrates his return home and his rediscovery of sea and land in Isla Negra, where he lived until

he died. But much of the optimism and serenity of the odes
are no longer present in this book. The poet is tormented by
spiritual and metaphysical problems and asks "permission to
be born again" ("pido permiso para nacer"). It is Neruda's
most personal book to date, written during what he called his
"autumnal" period. It is, therefore, a poetry of reflection
and maturity, wistful, exultant, somber and humorous, which
shows us not only the growth of the poet but the growth of
the whole person.

The book has been compared to Rubén Darío's Cantos
de vida y esperanza, since both poets are saddened in their
respective works by the irreversible progression of time toward death. [6] But what is lacking in Darío and present in
Neruda is the happiness that the latter finds in his "autumnal"
love:

> I only want five things,
> five chosen roots.
>
> One is an endless love.
>
> Two is to see the autumn.
> I cannot exist without leaves
> flying and falling to earth.
>
> The third is the solemn winter,
> the rain I loved, the caress
> of fire in the rough cold.
>
> My fourth is the summer,
> plump as a watermelon.
>
> And fifthly, your eyes.
> Matilde, my dear love,
> I will not sleep without your eyes,
> I will not exist but in your gaze. [7]

> Yo sólo quiero cinco cosas,
> cinco raíces preferidas.
>
> Una es el amor sin fin.
>
> Lo segundo es ver el otoño.
> No puedo ser sin que las hojas
> vuelen y vuelvan a la tierra.
>
> Lo tercero es el grave invierno,
> la lluvia que amé, la caricia
> del fuego en el frío silvestre.

En cuarto lugar el verano
redondo como una sandía.

La quinta cosa son tus ojos,
Matilde mía, bienamada,
no quiero dormir sin tus ojos,
no quiero ser sin que me mires [OC 1448].

Neruda's love for Matilde is reiterated throughout the book, but his most inspired song is included in "Autumn Testament," where he calls her "my chosen one," and tells her "I touched my blood in your mouth, / dear love, my Araucana":

What can I leave you, Matilde,
when you have at your touch
that aura of burning leaves,
that fragrance of strawberries,
and between your sea-breasts
the half-light of Cauquenes,
and the laurel-smell of Chile?[8]

Qué puedo dejarte si tienes,
Matilde Urrutia, en tu contacto
ese aroma de hojas quemadas,
esa fragancia de frutillas
y entre tus dos pechos marinos
el crepúsculo de Cauquenes
y el olor de peumo de Chile? [OC 1544].

The happiness of the love poetry is tainted with a shade of melancholy brought about by a reflection on the approaching hour of death. Neruda knows that in this autumnal period death is near, but he refuses to let the thought of death interfere with his love for Matilde. He even defies it: "but what good will it do us, / the closeness of a grave? / Let life not separate us; / and who cares about death?"[9]

Estravagario is a book that revolves in part around a tormented search for truth. Neruda no longer looks at things with the same clear understanding he had in the Odes. He sees reality and comprehends it, but he realizes that he is also capable of misrepresenting it. The falsity lies not in the things themselves, but in the way he perceives them. He tells us "all clarity is obscure," and this verse well characterizes the poetry of this period and his state of mind.

In "We Are Many," the subjective Neruda seems to look

upon his "alter ego" with skepticism, questioning what or who
he is:

> Of the many men who I am, who we are,
> I can't find a single one;
> they disappear among my clothes,
> they have left for another city.
>
> When everything seems to be set
> to show me off as intelligent,
> the fool I always keep hidden
> takes over all that I say.
>
> At other times, I'm asleep
> among distinguished people,
> and when I look for my brave self,
> a coward unknown to me
> rushes to cover my skeleton
> with a thousand fine excuses.
>
> When a decent house catches fire,
> instead of the fireman I summon,
> an arsonist bursts on the scene,
> and that's me.   What can I do?
> What can I do to distinguish myself?
> How can I pull myself together?
>
> All the books I read
> are full of dazzling heroes,
> always sure of themselves.
> I die with envy of them:
> and in films full of wind and bullets,
> I goggle at the cowboys,
> I even admire the horses.
>
> But when I call for a hero,
> out comes my lazy old self;
> so I never know who I am,
> nor how many I am or will be.
> I'd love to be able to touch a bell
> and summon the real me,
> because if I really need myself,
> I mustn't disappear.
>
> While I am writing, I am far away;
> and when I come back, I've gone.
> I would like to know if others
> go through the same things that I do,
> have as many selves as I have,
> and see themselves similarly;

and when I have exhausted this problem,
I am going to study so hard
that when I explain myself,
I will be talking geography. 10

De tantos hombres que soy, que somos,
no puedo encontrar a ninguno:
se me pierden bajo la ropa,
se fueron a otra ciudad.

Cuando todo está preparado
para mostrarme inteligente
el tonto que llevo escondido
se toma la palabra en mi boca.

Otras veces me duermo en medio
de la sociedad distinguida
y cuando busco en mí al valiente,
un cobarde que no conozco
corre a tomar con mi esqueleto
mil deliciosas precauciones.

Cuando arde una casa estimada
en vez del bombero que llamo
se precipita el incendiario
y ése soy yo. No tengo arreglo.
Qué debo hacer para escogerme?
Cómo puedo rehabilitarme?

Todos los libros que leo
celebran héroes refulgentes
siempre seguros de sí mismos:
me muero de envidia por ellos,
y en los films de vientos y balas
me quedo envidiando al jinete,
me quedo admirando al caballo.

Pero cuando pido al intrépido
me sale el viejo perezoso,
y así yo no sé quién soy,
no sé cuántos soy o seremos.
Me gustaría tocar un timbre
y sacar el mí verdadero
porque si yo me necesito
no debo desaparecerme.

Mientras escribo estoy ausente
y cuando vuelvo ya he partido:
voy a ver si a las otras gentes
les pasa lo que a mí me pasa,

si son tantos como soy yo,
si se parecen a sí mismos
y cuando lo haya averiguado
voy a aprender tan bien las cosas
que para explicar mis problemas
les hablaré de geografía [OC 1475-6].

Aside from being an amiable autobiographical sketch, "We Are Many" is a concise document regarding the many personalities of the poet and his continual search for identity. The basic interplay within the poem is between the Neruda writing the page and the literary Neruda, who reads books full of "dazzling heroes," and who dies "with envy of them"; between the Neruda who calls for a man of action and the "lazy old self" who unexpectedly appears.

This idea of duplicity is a key concept behind the poem. The relationship between the artist (creator) and his art (creation) is never simple and changes constantly, subject to innumerable adjustments and discriminations. But in order to learn who he is, the subjective Neruda must not allow the "other" to disappear.

As Neruda envisions the coming of winter (death), his search for truth centers around the problem of eternity. He interrogates priests, doctors, and learned men, but their answers are inconclusive. In the anticipation of nothingness, his verses become more desolate and he carries in his heart a "palpitation of dark stones." The poet, however, is not afraid of death, and death is no longer the great depriver, as it was in Residencia en la tierra. In his renewed vow of love for Matilde, Neruda is convinced that he and his beloved shall triumph over death:

Sometimes when we have stopped being,
stopped coming and going,
under seven blankets of dust
and the dry feet of death,
we will be close again, love ... [11]

Alguna vez si ya no somos,
si ya no vamos ni venimos
bajo siete capas de polvo
y los pies secos de la muerte,
estaremos juntos, amor ... [OC 1545].

In "Autumn Testament," which is the last poem of the

book, Neruda leaves a little of himself to everyone.   But
Estravagario, in its entirety, leaves us much more.   We
have a portrait of a poet who has matured and has learned
to accept his place in the world; a poet who reaffirms life
when confronted with death; a poet who has faith in humanity
and in himself; and a poet who has unceasing energy and unending love, even if the shadows of autumn occasionally
darken his interior landscape.

The clarity and simplicity of the Odes give way to a
more complex verse.   Still clear, but no longer transparent.
In Estravagario we have a poetry of contrasts where light
alternates with shadow, happiness with sadness, nostalgia
with vigor.   Rodríguez Monegal says of Neruda: "Ahora en
pleno otoño ha nacido de nuevo, dueño de su propia tiniebla"
("Now, in full autumn, he is born again, master of his own
shadows"). [12]

It is only logical, then, that Neruda should conclude
this "autumnal" poetry with a contemplation of himself.
While he is still writing Cantos ceremoniales (1961) and Plenos poderes (1962), he undertakes the task of recreating his
biography in prose and verse.   In January, 1962, he begins
to write in prose The Lives of the Poet, for the Brazilian
weekly O Cruzeiro. [13] These personal sketches inspire Memorial de Isla Negra, his spiritual biography in verse, and
later are included in his complete autobiography, Confieso
que he vivido, finished a few days before his death and published posthumously (see next chapter).

The Memorial de Isla Negra is comprised of five volumes: (1) Where the Rain Begins/Donde nace la lluvia; (2)
The Moon in the Labyrinth/La luna en el laberinto; (3) The
Cruel Fire/El cruel fuego; (4) The Root-Hunter/El cazador
de raíces; and (5) Critical Sonata/Sonata crítica; and is the
juxtaposition of various memories which come to represent
the poet's most intimate feelings.   As a result, it is not a
chronological account for the most part.

In a sense, the Memorial is more of a poetic diary
than it is autobiography.   It is the diary of the pensive poet,
who has a wonderful memory of his childhood and adulthood,
and who is inspired by his natural surroundings.   As such, it
contains all those things that may occur in the mind of a
writer as he is reflecting upon his life: the exquisite songs
on love, nature and art; the brooding on the mysteries; the
highly personal insights into the motives and affairs of people;
and the passionate musings on youth and age.

Where the Rain Begins, which documents the birth of
Neruda in 1904 and his trip to Santiago in 1921, is the most
autobiographical volume of the five.   It details the poet's
growing up between those years in a chronological succession.

The book's main theme centers around the biographical
roots of the poet: his early years and his first visit to his
mother in the cemetery; his relations with his stepmother and
his father; his encounter with the sea; his discovery of sexual
desire; his school years and his apprenticeship with poetry;
his preoccupations with the human condition, injustice and
superstition; and, finally, his insecurity in leaving his small
town for the capital, where he stays in a boarding house on
Maruri Street.

In "La mamadre," the stepmother is associated with
the goodness of bread.   She has raised the child with tenderness ever since his mother died.   In "El padre," Neruda remembers the austere figure of a man who conducts the trains
into the dark night.   His father's life is always in a state of
flux, as he comes and goes in his locomotive.   On the occasion of his father's death the poet remembers that "on a day
with more rain than any other day/ the conductor José del
Carmen Reyes/ boarded the train of death and has not returned" ("Un día con más lluvia que otros días/ el conductor
José del Carmen Reyes/ subió al tren de la muerte y hasta
ahora no ha vuelto").14*

In "El niño perdido," which may remind one of "We
Are Many," a more serious and concerned Neruda asks who
or what he was:

Slow childhood, out of which,
like long grass,
grows the hard pistil,
the wooden substance of man.

Who was I? What was I? What were we?

There is no answer.   We go through life.
We didn't go on being.   We were.   Other feet,
other hands, other eyes.
Everything experienced change, every leaf
in the tree.   And you?   Your skin changed,

---

*From this point on the fourth edition (1973) of the Obras
completas will be cited, as "OC4th," with volume and page
numbers, in the text.

your hair, your memory.   You were never
that other.
He was a boy who ran behind
the river, who passed on a bicycle,
in whose movement
your whole life passed at that moment.

Lenta infancia de donde
como de un pasto largo
crece el duro pistilo,
la madera del hombre.

Quién fui?   Qué fui?   qué fuimos?

No hay respuesta.   Pasamos.
No fuimos.   Éramos.   Otros pies,
otras manos, otros ojos.
Todo se fue mudando hoja por hoja
en el árbol.   Y en ti?   Cambió tu piel,
tu pelo, tu memoria.   Aquél no fuiste.
Aquél fue un niño que pasó corriendo
detrás de un río, de una bicicleta,
y con el movimiento
se fue tu vida con aquel minuto
        [OC4th, v2 p1039].

He imagines that his life is divided into watertight compart-
ments, and in each there is a different Neruda.   All these
different Nerudas never communicate with each other, don't
resemble each other, and are not responsible to each other.
The adolescent Neruda, for example, who arrives in Santiago
and is seduced by women who want to find in him someone
they have lost, is different from any other Neruda.   The
masks keep changing:

And we changed,
and never found out who we were;
at times we remembered
the one that lived in us,
and we asked him, perhaps, if he'd remember,
if he'd know at least that we were he, that
        we spoke
with his tongue;
but in the hours that passed
he looked at us, acknowledging nothing.

y cambiamos
y nunca más supimos quiénes éramos,

y a veces recordamos
al que vivió en nosotros
y le pedimos algo, tal vez que nos recuerde,
que sepa por los menos que fuimos él, que hablamos
con su lengua,
pero desde las horas consumidas
aquel nos mira y no nos reconoce [OC4th, v2 p1040].

The older Neruda recognizes the "persona" in the younger Neruda, but realizes that that part of his life is behind him and that everything has changed.

Donde nace la lluvia, or, literally, "Where the rain is born," is also where Neruda is born. From Parral, the boy moved to Temuco, where he spends his formative years. These two towns, and the constant rain, reveal the roots of the poet.

The second book of the sequence, The Moon in the Labyrinth, covers the years between 1921 and 1931, but not in a chronological order. During this time, the country boy has risen above his rural beginnings and has floundered out of his social depth. He has become a well-known poet and has been assigned a consular post in the Far East. The love he feels for two women, one from Temuco, the other, from Santiago, is contrasted with the disdain he feels for the hot lands of the Orient, beset with opium and death.

The first poems in the book are dedicated to Terusa and Rosaura, his two loves immortalized as Marisol and Marisombra in Veinte poemas de amor y una canción desesperada. There is also a poem dedicated to his friend and secretary Homero Arce Castillo, whom he calls brother. The last poems in the volume are devoted to his voyage to the Far East. It is the period in his life which corresponds to the writing of Residencia en la tierra. Neruda evokes a world in a state of disintegration and he sees, as in a mirror, the faithful reflection of a whole vanishing past.

In the third volume of Memorial, namely The Cruel Fire, Neruda reminisces about the Spanish Civil War, although only two poems are entirely devoted to this event. The rest of the book deals with the poet's years in the Orient, where he falls in love with Josie Bliss, and with a disparate collection of poems about the Cordillera de los Andes and the sea. As Neruda's stream of consciousness increases, chronology no longer seems to be important. His vision is focused instead on frustrated love and on the Chilean landscape.

Two poems deal with his passionate love for Josie
Bliss. But it is a love beset by stormy arguments and
jealousy. Josie Bliss is on a verge of a breakdown and
threatens to kill the poet with a knife. [15]

Perhaps the most lyrical poem in the book is "The
Tides," in which the poet feels he has come of age like
"mollusks in watery phosphor." Water, like the rain of previous poems, is a symbol for the plenitude of life. Reading
this poem carefully, one can't help but realize that Neruda's
poetry has also come of age.

In this volume, as well as in the next two, the autobiographical elements diminish as Neruda is more intent on
giving us a self-portrait. The author here is no longer the
melancholy poet bewailing the loss of an age of gold. He is
as silent and as revealing as the painter of a large canvas
representing a human being in the tumult of life. Even if he
is dealing with the past, it is an experience relived in the
present.

In The Root-Hunter, Neruda retraces his steps to the
period of the Spanish Civil War, then abruptly brings us to
the time of the Second World War, when he is in Mexico.
He declares his love for Alberto Sánchez, the sculptor friend
he met at the time of the Spanish Republic--and to whom the
book is dedicated, and for Delia del Carril, who did more
for him during and after the Guerra Civil than any other human being. Two of the best love poems of Memorial are
sung to her in this book.

In "Amores: Delia (I)," Neruda recalls the horrors
of the Spanish Civil War and is thankful to Delia for her love
and generosity as she accompanied him through that sorrowful
period. But he remembers most her gentleness:

> Delia is the light of the window open
> to truth, open to the honey-tree ...
> ...
> Delia, amid so many leaves
> in the tree of life,
> your presence
> in fire,
> your virtue
> in dew:
> in the irascible wind,
> a dove.

Delia es la luz de la ventana abierta
a la verdad, al árbol de la miel ...
. . .
Delia, entre tantas hojas
del árbol de la vida,
tu presencia
en el fuego,
tu virtud
de rocío:
en el viento iracundo
una paloma [OC4th, v2 1143-5].

And in "Amores: Delia (II)," he asks forgiveness if his relationship with her has not lasted. He wants her to know that
in spite of their separation, his love for her shall never
cease. "Nunca ha muerto una flor: sigue naciendo" ("Never
has a flower died: it keeps on being born") he tells her.
And adds:

Pardon my heart where
the noisy murmur of the bees dwells:
I know that you, like all beings,
touch the sublime honey,
and loosen
from the lunar stone, from the firmament,
your own star,
and that you are crystalline among all of them.

Perdón para mi corazón en donde
habita el gran rumor de las abejas:
yo sé que tú, como todos los seres,
la miel excelsa tocas
y desprendes
de la piedra lunar, del firmamento,
tu propia estrella,
y cristalina eres entre todas [OC4th, v2 1145].

The Root-Hunter begins with the image of the hunter
entering the forest. His boots are deep in the humid earth
and are looking for something. The hunter is, of course,
Neruda, and the roots he seeks represent immortality.

Critical Sonata, the last book of Memorial, is a diary
of the present. It is the most political of the five volumes
that make up the sequence and reminds us of the activist poet
concerned with those less fortunate than he is. In "Episode,"
for example, Neruda says:

My poetry is still a rainy road
where barefoot children pass to go to school
my only remedy is to remain silent:
if they give me a guitar, I shall sing
      bitter songs.

mi poesía es aún un camino en la lluvia
por donde pasan niños descalzos a la escuela
y no tengo remedio sino cuando me callo:
si me dan la guitarra canto cosas amargas
    [OC4th, v2 1169].

But the poetic material of the Critical Sonata is un-even, illustrating the political in his poem to Stalin "Episode," and the personal in "Solitude," where the poet reitirates that he is no longer the same.

The book ends with an ambiguous note, which indicates that the poet is preparing for death or that there will be more to his spiritual biography in verse:

Onward, let's leave
the suffocating river
where we navigate with other fish
from dawn to the migratory night,
and now in this discovered space
let's fly to pure solitude.

Adelante, salgamos
del río sofocante
en que con otros peces navegamos
desde el alba a la noche migratoria
y ahora en este espacio descubierto
volemos a la pura soledad [OC4th, v2 1197].

These are, then, the five books of Memorial de Isla Negra which have spoken most forcefully about Neruda's past, and have given us a self-portrait of the artist as he passes through life. Neruda's personal vision has clearly designated for him a history, a landscape and a state of mind, and no verse in any other book shows us a Neruda more conscious of his southern heritage. The expression of the personal in terms of the natural, the historical and the anecdotal, the translation of the objective into the more subjective, is characteristic not only of Neruda but of the great Spanish poets of the past, who sang without embarassment and without presumption.

Striving for simplicity in the Odes, Neruda shows a predilection for the small and a disavowal of the large. The composition is throughout made up of the tiny, the unpretentious, the concrete. As his poetry becomes more personal in Estravagario, the concrete alternates with the abstract, the extrinsic with the intrinsic. The poet is maturing and has realized that the light of the Odes was artificial and that he can no longer suppress the "dark roots of his song."[16] He now opens up his soul to show us the shadows as well as the transparency. In Memorial, the autobiographical serves as the background for a more intimate look at Neruda. We have a poetry of reflection and the poet himself is the object of that reflection. Neruda knows life precisely because he has experienced death--but death no longer imposes the terror of imminent non-being, as it did in Residencia en la tierra. Through the period of some ten years, his poetry has represented the joy of the material world and the psychological and spiritual growth of the self.

From the Odes to Memorial we have seen two unequal and distinct poetic endeavors. They are, first, the poetry that furnished the action with a universe of small, fresh, lifelike details--as we find in the Odes; and, second, the poetry that portrays the personal--as we find in Estravagario and in Memorial. Although Neruda's intent to write for the simple folk was the same in all these works, it is sufficient to read poems such as "Lazybones" (Estravagario) or "Future in Space" (Memorial) to see that he does not always succeed.

In conclusion, we can say that Neruda's evolution toward a simpler form has had partial results: the poet who wanted to reach the masses in the Odes, and succeeded to a large extent, probably remains sealed from them in his later works. In both Estravagario and Memorial de Isla Negra, the quality of aloofness which characterized his earlier poetry is in no way diminished; indeed, the symbols--although less numerous--are at times more dense, more novel, and richer in their combinations and modulations, without a hint that the reader is any less the outsider than he was during the obscure phase of Neruda's writings.

VI

THE MEMOIRS

The Memoirs of Pablo Neruda are more like "notebooks" than memoirs. They remind us of Rainer Maria
Rilke's The Notebooks of Malte Laurids Brigge for their in-
formal style containing recollections which are not deliberate
and which spring from memory unshaped. Like Rilke's work,
the Memoirs are too personal and original to be classified
under any fixed genre. Although all the material is autobiographical, Neruda makes a distinction at the beginning of the
book between what the biographer remembers and what the
poet remembers:

> These memoirs or recollections are intermittent and
> often full of gaps because life is precisely the same
> way. The interval of sleep allows us to sustain the
> days of toil. Many of my reminiscences have faded
> as I have tried to evoke them, and have turned to dust
> like an irrevocably shattered crystal.
> The memoirs of the biographer are not the me-
> moirs of the poet. The former lived probably less
> but photographed a lot more, and entertains us with
> a profusion of details. The latter, hands us a gal-
> lery of phantasms shaken by the fire and by the
> darkness of his age.
> It is likely that I did not live within my self;
> that I lived the lives of others.
> From all that I have written on these pages
> three will always remain--as in the trees of autumn
> and as in the ripening of the vines--the yellow leaves
> which are dying and the grapes which will find a new
> life in the sacred wine.
> My life is a life made up of all those lives: the
> lives of the poet.

> Esta memorias o recuerdos son intermitentes y a

Pablo Neruda and Matilde Urrutia in 1972. (Photograph by
Sara Facio-Alicia D'Amico Fotografías, Buenos Aires; used
with permission.)

ratos olvidadizos porque así precisamente es la vida. La intermitencia del sueño nos permite sos-
tener los días de trabajo. Muchos de mis recuer-
dos se han desdibujados al evocarlos, han devenido
en polvo como un cristal irremediablemente herido.
      Las memorias del memorialista no son las me-
morias del poeta. Aquél vivió tal vez menos, pero
fotografió más y nos recrea con la pulcritud de los
detalles. Éste nos entrega una galería de fantasmas sacudidos por el fuego y la sombra de su
época.
      Tal vez no viví en mí mismo; tal vez viví la
vida de los otros.
      De cuanto he dejado escrito en estas páginas se
desprenderán siempre--como en las arboledas de
otoño y como en el tiempo de las viñas--las hojas
amarillas que van a morir y las uvas que revivirán
en el vino sagrado.
      Mi vida es una vida hecha de todas las vidas:
las vidas del poeta.[1]*

The Lives of the Poet were ten long autobiographical
pieces which Neruda wrote for O Cruzeiro Internacional, in
1962, on the theme of life and poetry. It wasn't until ten
years later, however, when he returned to Chile from his
ambassadorial post in Paris, that he decided to turn the original into a complete and coherent volume of memoirs. The
result is a book of quiet, close-knit prose, full of unforget-
table scenes, and set forth in precise, analytical descriptions,
which at times become lyrical flights of near-poetry (see "El
bosque chileno"/"The Chilean Forest" as an example). It is
uniquely Neruda and touches the reader with the same sudden
revelations and uncanny awareness as do his poems.

In the 12 notebooks (cuadernos) that comprise the Memoirs, Neruda recalls his childhood and various stages of his
life, and describes his thoughts and sensations with extraordinary suggestiveness. He muses on the meaning of life and
death, showing his familiarity with the temples of Eastern
wisdom, and develops many themes which we have come to

---

*From this point on all references to the Memoirs will be
designated as "M," followed by the page number, and will be
incorporated into the text. For an excellent translation of this
work see Pablo Neruda, Memoirs (New York: Farrar, Straus
and Giroux, 1977), translated by Hardy St. Martin.

recognize as most characteristic of Neruda: poetry, love, friendship, politics. All of these themes show us a profound-ly self-revealing poet.

Yet the Memoirs disclose another aspect of the writ-er; that he is "an irresistible storyteller."2 With him, we embark on a picaresque adventure, which begins with his childhood and ends with an account of a tragic event in Chile: the military coup. *

Pablo Neruda has always been an autobiographical poet. In the first cuaderno, titled "Country Boy," he recalls his early years and his love for poetry. He was eight when he wrote his first poem, timidly approaching his stepmother and his father to show it to them. They were engaged in a discussion in a low voice and paid little attention to him. Fi-nally his father glanced at the poem and asked him: "Where did you copy it from?" (M 20). Years afterwards, fearing the wrath of an unreceptive father, who hated poets and had already burned some of his notebooks, he began using the pen name Pablo Neruda. He was 16, and had copied the surname of Czechoslovak writer Jan Neruda (1834-91) from a maga-zine.

Throughout his life, Neruda had advocated an earthy poetry of experience, a sensuous poetry,

> steeped in sweat and smoke, smelling of lilies and urine ... a poetry impure as the clothing we wear, or our bodies, soup-stained, soiled with our shame-ful behavior, our wrinkles and vigils and dreams, observations and prophecies, declarations of loathing and love, idyls and beasts, the shocks of encounter, political loyalties, denial and doubts, affirmation and taxes. 3

Once, Neruda tells us, a Uruguayan critic was shocked because he had compared stones to small ducks in his Odas elementales. Furious at the critic for having established that small ducks and some other kind of small animals were not material for poetry, he retorted:

---

*As all friends of Chile know, the Chilean generals who mur-dered Socialist President Salvador Allende Gossens struck on September 11, 1973. The coup had an adverse effect on the precarious health of the poet, who died a few days later.

> Literary refinement has come to this lack of serious-
> ness. They are obliging creative artists to deal
> only with sublime themes. But they are mistaken.
> We shall make poetry even out of those things most
> scorned by the professors of good taste.

> A esta falta de seriedad ha llegado el verbococo
> literario. Quieren obligar a los creadores a no tra-
> tar sino temas sublimes. Pero se equivocan. Ha-
> remos poesía hasta con las cosas más despreciadas
> por los maestros del bueno gusto [M 398].

As we follow the chronology of the poet, we see that
he projects different personalities in his writings. Each distinct period seems to produce another poet, expressing his
most current feelings, impressions and thoughts. He considers his first literary achievement to be the love letters
he wrote to Blanca Wilson, and intuited that "perhaps love
and nature were from the very beginnings the foundations of
my poetry" ("Tal vez el amor y la naturaleza fueron desde
muy temprano los yacimientos de mi poesía") (M 21).

In Crepusculario, we have a poet who feels like a lost
boy in a hostile city, where he suffers from hunger and
shivers through the harsh winters. He tells us that El hondero entusiasta was written in a fit of inspiration: he looked at
the sky and was dazzled by a lively multitude of swarming
stars. After getting star drunk, cosmically drunk, he describes how: "I ran to my table, in a delirious state, and
wrote--as if I were taking a dictation--the first poem of the
book" ("Corrí a mi mesa y escribí de manera delirante, como
si recibiera un dictado, el primer poema de un libro") (M 69).

While he was still in Santiago, Neruda wrote his famous Veinte poemas de amor y una canción desesperada,
which sold more than a million copies throughout the world.
Neruda refers to it as:

> a pastoral and painful book that contains my most
> tormented adolescent passions, mixed with the de-
> vastating nature of the South. It is a book I love
> because in spite of its acute melancholy, the joy of
> being alive is present in it.

> un libro doloroso y pastoril que contiene mis más
> atormentadas pasiones adolescentes, mezcladas con
> la naturaleza arrolladora del sur de mi patria. Es

un libro que amo porque a pesar de su aguda melan-
colía está presente en él el gozo de la existencia
[M 70].

In "Criticism and Self Criticism," Neruda refers to
two of his most misunderstood books: Residencia en la tierra, with its darkness and gloom, and Las uvas y el viento,
with its abundant light and vast spaces.   He tells us that both
books have a right to exist within his works.   He speaks with
affection of other books: España en el corazón, Canto general, Odas elementales, Los versos del capitán, and Estravagario, calling the latter his most intimate book.   Looking back
at Residencia en la tierra, he cannot forget that a youth from
Santiago killed himself at the foot of a tree, with the book
open at the poem "Significa sombras" ("It Means Shadows").
But of all the books mentioned, he has a soft spot in his heart
for Las uvas y el viento, written when the poet set wandering
through the world:

> It contains the dust of roads and the waters of
> rivers; it contains peoples, communities, places
> overseas which were unknown to me until I dis-
> covered them in my travels.
>
> Tiene polvo de caminos y agua de ríos; tiene seres,
> continuidades y ultramar de otros sitios que yo no
> conocía y que me fueron revelados de tanto andar
> [M 397].

Although we see in these works different poets molded
by the experience of the moment, all the poets are the poet.
What these diverse books have in common is the way the poem
is fashioned by the artist.   As Victor Howes has stated, "to
Neruda, writing a poem is a physical act, describable in
verbs of motion."[4] He quotes Neruda saying:

> I run after certain words.... I catch them in mid-
> air, as they buzz past, I trap them, clean them,
> peel them, I set myself in front of the dish, they
> have a crystalline texture to me, vibrant, ivory,
> vegetable, oily, like fruit, like algae, like agates,
> like olives.... And I stir them, I shake them, I
> drink them, I gulp them down, I mash them, I gar-
> nish them, I let them go....[5]

While it is impossible to characterize Neruda's verse
in a few pages, the reader will at once discover the elegant

music of the poet's voice as he himself describes the traits of his poetry:

> My poetry is becoming a material part of an infinitely vast environment, at times submarine and subterraneous, and is entering through galleries of extraordinary vegetation, conversing in daylight with solar phantasms, exploring the secret mineral caves hidden in the earth, determining the forgotten relations of autumn and man. The atmosphere becomes obscure and, on occasion, clears with lightning charged with phosphorescence and terror; a new construction, distant from the most obvious, worn-out words, appears in the skyline; a new continent is raised from the most secret essence of my poetry. In populating these lands, classifying this kingdom, touching all its mysterious shores, pacifying its foam, rerunning its zoology and its longitudinal geography, I have spent obscure, solitary and remote years.

> Mi poesía comienza a ser parte material de un ambiente infinitamente espacial, de un ambiente a la vez submarino y subterráneo, a entrar por galerías de vegetación extraordinaria, a conversar a pleno día con fantasmas solares, a explorar la cavidad del mineral escondido en el secreto de la tierra, a determinar las relaciones olvidadas del otoño y del hombre. La átmosfera se oscurece y la aclaran a veces relámpagos recargados de fosforescencia y de terror; una nueva construcción lejos de las palabras más evidentes, más gastadas, aparece en la superficie del aire; un nuevo continente se levanta de la más secreta materia de mi poesía. En poblar estas tierras, en clasificar este reino, en tocar sus orillas misteriosas, en apaciguar su espuma, en recorrer su zoología y su geográfica longitud, he pasado años oscuros, solitarios y remotos [M 204].

He adds:

> My poetry and my life have advanced like an American river, like a torrent of Chilean waters born in the most secret depths of the southern mountains, ceaselessly directing its currents toward the sea. My poetry did not reject anything that could be caught

in the flow; it accepted passion, unraveled mysteries
and worked its way into the heart of the people.

My poesía y mi vida han transcurrido como un río
americano, como un torrente de aguas de Chile,
nacidas en la profundidad secreta de las montañas
australes, dirigiendo sin cesar hacia una salida marina el movimiento de sus corrientes. Mi poesía
no rechazó nada de lo que pudo traer en su caudal;
aceptó la pasión, desarrolló el misterio, y se
abrió paso entre los corazones del pueblo [M 235-6].

In the Latin American tradition, Neruda's poems se-
cure him a number of consular posts that take him to Burma, Ceylon, Java, Singapore, Argentina, Spain and Mexico.
Between his travels and his consular duties, his poetic contribution is substantial. What is equally as impressive, however, is the fact that Neruda has made people respect the
occupation of the poet and the profession of poetry.

Covering this period, the Memoirs also reveal the development of a human being. The poet/diplomat starts deep
in misery when at the age of 23 he finds himself in Rangoon,
without money or friends, and gradually reaches consolation
and even happiness as he discovers the mysteries of love in
the Orient.

The theme of love permeates many of these pages.
Perhaps the stormiest relation the poet has is with Josie
Bliss, a Burmese who likes to pass for an English woman.
She is evoked as an apparition out of the past that comes to
haunt the poet with memories of intense sensual experiences
and jealousy. Neruda calls her an "amorous terrorist," and
laments that her tempestuous temper thwarted their relationship. When he abandons her in Rangoon, without saying good-
bye, he feels guilty and later writes her a beautiful poem
"El tango del viudo" ("The Widower Tango"). He sails for
Colombo, Ceylon, to take over a new consulate, thinking that
he will never see her again. He is wrong. Josie, madly in
love, has pursued him, appearing one morning at his house.

The love which was achieved at the height of fate's
rising cycle was suddenly destroyed by the downward cycle,
the cycle that according to Eastern tradition brings sorrow.
After a short reunion in Colombo, the lovers acknowledge that
their tormented relationship cannot continue. Neruda accompa-
nies Josie Bliss to the ship that will take her back to Burma,

and sees her leave with a heavy heart.   In a last desperate
act, Josie throws herself at the poet's feet and kisses his
white shoes, smearing the chalk polish all over her face.

There are other references in Neruda's journals to
women and love.   More often than not, however, these loves
remain nameless.   Neruda remembers, for example, one of
his first sexual encounters in a secluded ranch where he
sleeps with eight other men in a haystack.   Unexpectedly, a
naked body approaches him and begins to feel him.   He reci-
procates and makes love to a woman he never sees.   The
next day, he scrutinizes the women in the ranch and sees
one of them smiling, an older woman probably married to a
rancher.   When he is in the Orient, many women come to
his cot and leave, always remaining anonymous.

An exception is Maria Antonieta (Maruca) Agenaar, a
Dutch woman with some Malay blood.   Neruda's solitude in
the Orient increases and he decides to marry her.   But we
learn little about this marriage, and even less about the death
of their only daughter (and Neruda's only child) in Paris.

The theme of love is expressed with unsurpassed lyricism when Neruda reminisces about Delia in Spain and
France and Matilde in Mexico and Italy.   Delia is the "sweet-
est passenger, thread of steel and honey who lived with me
during my most productive years" ("pasajera suavísima, hilo
de acero y miel que ató mis manos en los años sonoros")
(M 295).   Nevertheless, he remembers her only in passing.
To Matilde, he writes a touching short passage where he refers to her country origins: "From the earth, with feet and
hands and eyes and voice, she brought to me all the roots,
all the flowers, all the fragrant fruits of happiness" ("De la
tierra, con pies y manos y ojos y voz, trajo para mí todas
las raíces, todas las flores, todos los frutos fragrantes de
la dicha") (M 373).   Matilde is an integral part of the natural
world, and shares with Pablo its magical powers.

In the pages written on love, there are many allusions
to sexual intercourse, but the language and imagery used by
Neruda never let the reader forget the spiritual implications
of his physical love.

Friends, lovers, acquaintances surface and disappear
in the Memoirs.   Neruda is a master of the anecdotal.
Whether his friends are writers, poets, painters, muralists,
or politicians, they are his fellow pilgrims on a quest to re-

assert the values of humanity and humanism. The friends he
is closest to are his brothers; others, a shade less intimately, his confrères. The list is long and incomplete. Neruda
embraces all, the influential people and the scoundrels, the
aristocrats and the servants. He even feels great affection
for Kruzi, a mongoose who followed him home one day in
Burma to later accompany him across the Bay of Bengal to
Ceylon. His relationships are relaxed and numerous, some
veiled with secrecy (as was his affair with Matilde when he
was still living with Delia), some open and honest (as was his
brief comradeship with Federico García Lorca). What they
have in common is that everything bears the scent of warm
intimacy.

Neruda recalls Alvaro, his scoundrel friend, who ac-
companies the poet to his first consular post in Rangoon.
Together they seduce women on the boat crossing from America to Europe, get drunk in bars, follow the sexual rituals of
the houses of prostitution, and live a picaresque existence,
often in need of money. Neruda has fond recollections of this
"conquistador," who leaves one day never to return, probably
fulfilling his desire of settling in New York City.

The tenderest memories are of Federico García Lorca
with whom he gives a humorous lecture on Rubén Darío in
Buenos Aires. From Argentina, Neruda is sent to Spain,
where he renews his friendship with García Lorca. There he
meets other writers and artists, some of whom will be devoted to him for life (Rafael Alberti among them). When
García Lorca is shot, anger flows from Neruda's pen.

A consular assignment takes the poet to Mexico, where
he meets and befriends the great muralists: Diego Rivera,
José Clemente Orozco, David Alfaro Siqueiros. Then he goes
to Paris, where he gets into trouble with the French police for
lack of proper documentation, and is helped immensely by
Pablo Picasso.

An unwitting incident begins a lifelong friendship with
Soviet writer Ilya Ehrenburg, who subsequently translates
most of his works into Russian. Neruda and Delia were escaping the persecution of the González Videla Government in
Chile when they arrived in Paris (Neruda was using the passport of his friend Miguel Angel Asturias, whom he resembled).
It seemed that wherever Neruda went, the Chilean Government
harassed him, asking other governments to make things difficult for him. In the French capital, the Sûreté had a file
which said:

Neruda and his wife Delia del Carril make frequent
trips to Spain, carrying Soviet instructions.   They
receive them from the Russian writer Ilya Ehrenburg, with whom Neruda also makes clandestine
trips to Spain.   To keep in close contact with Ehrenburg, Neruda has even rented and moved into an
apartment in the same building where the Soviet
writer lives.

Neruda y su mujer, Delia del Carril, hacen fre-
cuentes viajes a España, llevando y trayendo instrucciones soviéticas.   Las instrucciones las re-
ciben del escritor ruso Ilya Ehrenburg con el que
también Neruda hace viajes clandestinos a España.
Neruda, para establecer un contacto más privado
con Ehrenburg, ha alquilado y se ha ido a vivir a
un departamento situado en el mismo edificio que
habita el escritor soviético [M 259].

The file, presumably sent by the Chilean authorities in Paris,
had been dispatched to the Quai d'Orsay and was brought to
Neruda's attention by a friend, Jean Richard Bloch, who knew
a functionary at the Ministry of Foreign Relations.   The
functionary was working on Neruda's deportation.

Seeing that he was being expelled from France on the
"wildest assumptions," Neruda decides to protest.   The Ministry, however, does little to investigate the matter and allows
the absurd charges against him to stand (M 259).

As it turns out, Neruda didn't even know Ehrenburg
at the time.   He decides to meet him and finds him having a
late lunch at La Coupole.   "I am Pablo Neruda, the poet
from Chile," he says.   "According to the French police, we
are close friends ... we even live in the same building."
Seeing a surprised Ehrenburg, Neruda adds: "Since I am being deported on account of you, I wish to meet you and, at
least, shake your hand."   Ehrenburg replies: "I also wanted
to meet you, Neruda."   Neruda thinks that it was on that
same day that Ehrenburg decided to translate into Russian España en el corazón.   He says that, unintentionally, the French
police provided him with one of the most pleasant friendships
he ever had (M 260).

Neruda has tender memories of other poets he met in
Europe.   Prominent among them we find Paul Eluard and
Pierre Reverdy, from France, and Salvatore Quasimodo, from

Italy. He calls Eluard "magnificent" for his clear style and
his concern and strong ties with the people of France during
the years of Nazi occupation; he mourns the death of Reverdy,
a poet who was convinced that the world was drowning in a
flood tide of books; and he says that Quasimodo is the perfect
example of the universal man, praising his tight language, his
classicism and his romanticism.

Neruda remembers the past with extraordinary evoca-
tions of persons and places, from Gandhi and the young Nehru
to Jerzy Borejsza, a Polish poet, André Malraux, Spanish
poets and artists, and Chinese and Soviet leaders he met in
his travels. Recalling the chill of a Moscow winter, he calls
the Russian capital a "huge winter palace, " where the snow
glitters on "infinitely repeated roofs. "[6] Neruda is pleased
that Mao Tse-tung holds his hand longer than customary, and
that Nehru thinks of him as an emissary of peace. Turning to
Ghandi, he characterizes him as a very "cunning fox, " not unlike the Latin American "caciques" (creole leaders). Finally,
he honors Fidel Castro and Ernesto (Che) Guevara for their
role in the Cuban Revolution.

Before closing the page on friendship, Neruda pays
tribute to Gabriela Mistral, César Vallejo, Vicente Huidobro
and contemporary novelists who have given so much credibili-
ty and prominence to Latin America: Miguel Ángel Asturias,
Jorge Amado, Mario Vargas Llosa, José Donoso, Julio Cor-
tázar, and the irreverent Gabriel García Márquez. At the
same time, he praises Elías Laferte, the old Chilean Communist leader, and two Chilean presidents whose terms of
office were interrupted by violent death: José Manuel Balma-
ceda Fernández and Salvador Allende Gossens.

Neruda's Memoirs could not pass over in silence the
serious difficulties of de-Stalinization. In 1954 Neruda had
admired Joseph Stalin, calling him "the high noon, the maturity of men and peoples. "[7] But by 1963 his assessment of
the Soviet leader had completely changed. Neruda portrayed
him then as a cruel man, responsible for the death of many
people.

The poet's repudiation of Stalin, however, is not a repudiation of Communism. Since the Spanish Civil War Neruda
had been happy to be a Communist and viewed his art as an
instrument of change.

The mercurial world of Latin American politics runs

like a tangled thread in the life of the poet. His hopes to put
an end to the tortuous search for social justice and political
stability are followed by betrayals, assassination, and finally
the coup d'état.

The inhumanity of the military takeover shocks him out
of his peaceful existence in Isla Negra, where he had shut
himself from the rest of the world in order to finish his book
of Memoirs. These events provide him with the dominant political themes found in the last few pages of the book.

Although we have noted the changes rung by time
throughout Neruda's long period of creativity, the coup provides a drastic change within the Memoirs themselves. The
lyrical prose used to evoke his poetic beginnings, his love affairs, and his wonderful friendships, turns into violent language that attempts to capture the historic mood of the moment. In a tone reminiscent of the angry poet of España en
ˆ corazón, Neruda damns the politicians and the generals who
ᴸave sold their country to the interests of the oligarchy and
the foreigners. He depicts them as corrupt and sordid, and
totally lacking in moral fiber.

Most of all, Neruda mourns the death of his friend
Allende and gives an emotional account of the first three days
of the coup. Perhaps because of a presentiment about his
own death, he ends the Memoirs with the image of a corpse
followed to an unknown graveyard only by a woman "who carries with her the grief of the world" (M 469).

Even though the Memoirs leave out important details
about Neruda's life, and are covered with dull patches which
tell us about political quarrels, banquets, prizes, readings,
and poetic gratifications, they are impregnated with humanity
and lyrical passages. The hand is Neruda's.

Two weeks after the coup, death surprised him with
a notebook full of topics he had not had time to expand or
edit. The final editing of the book was done by Matilde Urrutia and Miguel Otero Silva, his Venezuelan friend who prepared the manuscript for publication.

In a conversation she had with Jorge Edwards, who
served in the Chilean Embassy in Paris when Neruda was the
ambassador of the Salvador Allende's government, Matilde Urrutia told him how her husband spent the last days (see chapter VIII for a detailed account of Neruda's death). On Sep-

tember 14 Neruda was lying in his sickbed and was dictating the final pages of the Memoirs, in which he describes the attack on the Presidential Palace (La Moneda) and the death of Allende.   Suddenly, the soldiers of the junta forcibly entered their house in Isla Negra.   Matilde told the army commander to begin the search with the poet's bedroom.   Neruda was shaken but received the soldiers cordially; he even offered them something to drink, which they declined.   As he saw that they were intimidated by his presence, he told them: "Search everything.   You will find nothing.   Yet I warn you that there is something here very dangerous for you: Poetry!"[8]

Neruda's Memoirs complement his autobiographical poetry.   Both give us a writer who shows himself to be a poet and storyteller who, like Cervantes, was not of an age but for all time.

VII

REMEMBERING PABLO:
CONVERSATIONS WITH HORMIGA

Her face conveys serenity and hope. Her figure is
fragile and graceful. Her walk is difficult, the result of a
serious accident which broke her pelvis years ago. Her
voice is musical and shows off a woman of intelligence and
charm. Her work is herself. It consists, of course, of
painting, drawing, printing. In Moscow and Paris, Lima
and Caracas, Madrid and Buenos Aires, her exhibits have
been accepted triumphantly, and she has been acclaimed as
an outstanding developer of the graphic arts. She recalls that
she has painted "since always." During the last few years,
she has been drawing horses: robust and unrestrained, suffering and subdued, impetuous and regal, but always with a
quasi-human quality. She is an artist who continues to draw
from life itself. This attractive nonagenarian, thin and pe-
tite, with pink cheeks and brown eyes, has a gentle, rather
fussy manner. On close scrutiny, her brown eyes often have
a little twinkle in them. Her name is Delia del Carril, and
she is known to her friends as "Hormiga" or "Hormiguita."
For 19 years (1934-1952) she lived with Pablo Neruda, and
remembers him with great tenderness.

When they met in Spain, in 1934, Hormiga was acquainted with the most refined intellectual circles of Madrid.
Her closest friends included humanists, poets, artists: Federico García Lorca, Pablo Picasso, Miguel Hernández, Rafael Alberti. Because she was always helpful to others, especially during the first months of the Civil War, Luis Enrique Delano, Acario Cotapos, and other friends began to
call her "Hormiguita," literally "little ant." The explanation
was that, like an ant, she always carried on her shoulder a
load greater than her weight. It was her generosity that attracted Pablo to her. When Neruda married her, he said
that "he had found in Delia that which all his other friends
put together could not give him."

138

Delia del Carril in her studio in Santiago, 1970's (photograph
by Bob Borowicz; used with permission).

With conditions in Spain as they were, it is not surprising that Neruda, surrounded by Republican sympathizers,
should begin to write a poetry of protest, and that he should
become converted slowly to Communism.   Delia, who already belonged to the Party, was delighted.   It is clear from
her recollections that she wielded a great deal of influence in
the political education of her husband.

I met Delia del Carril through Monica Schmidt de
Hoyos, a mutual friend of many years. It was April, 1975,
and I had been invited to a dinner at Delia's house. I was
not surprised to see that she still counted on an important
circle of friends, who very religiously prepared sumptuous

meals for her every Friday night. * During my two-month
stay in Chile, I became part of the group, having the good
fortune of entertaining extended conversations with Delia on
Pablo Neruda and his work.   My visits were frequent and
we spoke freely.   Notwithstanding this, Hormiga refused to
let me tape our conversations, afraid that the tapes might
fall into the hands of the Chilean military and cause all sorts
of problems for her friends.   What follows is a brief sketch
of Delia del Carril and some recollections of our dialogues,
which were scribbled down in a notebook.

Delia del Carril was born into a wealthy Argentinian
family of landowners in the 1880's.   She spent half of her
childhood in Europe, where she received most of her education and, for a while, flirted with the thought of becoming a
nun in a Spanish convent.   As a young woman, she became
familiar with the "other" Spain.   But it was Republican Spain
she adored.   After a brief stint as a voice student in the
famous school of Madame Batori ("I could sing magnificently
in the workers' choir, yet I was never able to sing alone in
front of an audience"), she pursued her apprenticeship of art
in the ateliers of André Lhote and Fernand Léger.   It was
the latter that worked closely with her and greatly influenced
her style.   He was often heard saying to her: "What did I
do?"   "Now you do it!"

The magnetic and sophisticated studio of Stanley Wil-
liam Hayter in Paris was instrumental in the development of
her techniques.   But it wasn't until 1954, after her separation
from Neruda, that she began devoting her time solely to painting and print-making.   She joined the renowned Santiago ate-
lier, Taller 99, directed by the able Nemesio Antúnez, who
insisted that she persevere in her art and that she develop
her own style.   Today, strong black lines delineate the bodies
of horses and human beings that represent the dominant themes
of her work.

Delia del Carril and I first began talking about Pablo
Neruda after an early dinner in May, at which we drank to

---

*Among them, professors Emilio Ellena and Arnoldo de Hoy-
os, Roser Bru, Dinora, Eduardo Vilches, Florencia de Ames-
ti (artists from the Taller 99), Doctor Pedro Castillo, who
had been ministers of health in the Allende government, and
various diplomats from South America and Eastern and Western Europe.

the health of Luis Corvalán (the Secretary General of the
Chilean Communist Party who was in jail and had just been
awarded the Lenin Prize for peace).   Comfortably ensconced
in the living room of her old house, which Pablo, as was
customary, had helped build, we began discussing such topics
as the years in Spain, the death of Federico García Lorca,
their brief residence in France to organize a worldwide congress of writers concerned with the Civil War, the years of
persecution by the Chilean government when both were fugitives, and, to a lesser extent, their separation.   We also
talked briefly about some of Neruda's books.   By the time I
was ready to leave Chile we had covered all of those topics
(some, of course, with more depth than others).   As is understandable, Hormiga refused to discuss the current political situation in Chile, although it was clear that her sympa-
thies were with Allende.   What appears here as a single interview is, in fact, the compendium of many hours of talk
(May, 1975).

*   *   *

S. B.   Hormiguita, we have been talking about your
life and art.   I would like to discuss now the years you spent
with Pablo.

D. C.   I met Pablo in Madrid, in 1934.   Gabriela Mistral was at the time consul in Madrid.   Because of some serious misunderstanding with Spanish officials, she decided to
return home and Pablo was recalled from Barcelona to take
her place.   Things were very intense in Spain.   The Republicans had recently come to power through democratic elections
and had set up a popular government, not unlike the Unidad
Popular (Allende's) government in Chile.

I was studying art at the San Fernando Academy in
Madrid when Pablo arrived from the coastal city.   He was
received with great enthusiasm by his writer and artist friends,
who were also mine.

Pablo had always been close to Federico [García Lor-
ca].   After our marriage, they would see each other on a daily basis.   You can imagine the shock we experienced when we
found out that Federico had been shot.   In a sense, the brothers Panero were at fault, although indirectly.   Federico was
safe in Madrid, but they insisted that he go to Granada.
There he was received by intimate friends, the Rosales, who

were Falangists. They wanted to save Federico, yet they did
not know how. The news of his death made everyone cry.
I remember how María Teresa Léon [Rafael Alberti's wife]
cried. She could not stop. Federico had always shied away
from the aristocracy and directed his energies toward the
people. Pablo did the same. They were as close as two
brothers.

During his two-year stay in Spain, from the inception
of the Republican government to the outbreak of the Civil War,
Pablo became increasingly interested in politics. The profound
social, political and economic changes inside Spain were arous-
ing opposition in fascist Europe and in the United States.
Within Spain itself, a polarization of leftist and rightist forces
occurred, revealing the most severe political and social cleav-
age found in any Western country since the French Revolution.
Within days, all of Spain was divided into two warring camps.
As a result, it became more and more difficult for Pablo as
Chilean consul to maintain neutrality. A few months after the
war began, he was asked to return to Chile.

By this time Spain was in great turmoil. It was very
sad having to leave so many friends behind. Before the trip
back home, Pablo decided to go to Paris. At the invitation
of French authors, he was to organize the Latin American
writers for a worldwide congress to be held in Madrid. Its
purpose was to awaken the consciousness of people throughout
the world and make them focus on the terrible strife that was
tearing the Spanish nation apart.

As we were leaving Madrid, we passed by a toy store.
Pablo stopped and began looking at a sailboat in the window.
I reminded him that we did not have much time left, but he
paid no attention to me. He kept staring at the boat, totally
seduced by its beauty and craftsmanship. Resolutely, he entered the store and inquired about the price of the toy. He
could not afford it. He never carried money. Money was
not important to him. One look at me and I knew what he
was thinking. Pablo left for France. Alone. I had to go
back home and joined him in the French capital a few days
later, with the boat under my arm.

S.B. Did that annoy you?

D.C. Not in the least. Artists, all artists, should be
serious about their work, but not about themselves. Pablo was
like a child. And I loved him for it. Picasso was the same

way, and he was much older.   All sensitive people have a
little of the child in themselves.   Once they lose that quality, they have nothing to live for.   When Pablo liked something, he had to have it.   It did not matter how much it cost.
Many times he would visit a friend's house and his eyes
would rest on a beautiful object.   Very cunningly, he would
talk about its virtues, would fondle it, would contemplate it,
until the friend, with some embarrassment, would offer it to
him.   Pablo would be reluctant at first, but would always accept it.   It wasn't long before his friends learned to put
away their dearest possessions when Pablo visited them.

S. B.   Hormiguita, returning to our discussions about
France, how did the organization of Latin American writers,
and the Congress [of anti-Fascist writers] turn out?   It is
my understanding that Pablo had differences with César Vallejo (Peruvian poet) and Vicente Huidobro (Chilean poet).

D. C.   First of all let me set you straight on this.
César and Pablo were always good friends.   They had their
disagreements, but they were always resolved in a civil way.
Pablo liked César very much, for his poetry and for the fact
that they both had Indian blood.   César's wife was very bour-
geois.   She used to count how many sugar cubes César put in
his coffee and reprimand him if they were too many.   She
was unbearable.   César rented an apartment without her
knowledge and began living with another woman.   Since he
was poor, things were not going too well for him.   Pablo
tried to help him, but he was too proud to accept his help.
That is where they disagreed.   Not that Pablo had a lot of
money.   His salary had been cut off by the Chilean government when he was recalled.   Like César, he had to live on
the meager salary apportioned him by the French writers.

With Huidobro, things were different.   He and Pablo
had a falling out and were not speaking to each other.   The
reason for this was that Huidobro had circulated a nasty poem
about Pablo in Spain.   Vicente Aleixandre got so mad that he
burned it.   But Pablo has never spoken ill of a rival poet.
It was Huidobro who filled César's head with stories about
Pablo.   In a heated conversation between Pablo and César
everything was cleared up.   The two continued to be friends.

In bringing together so many writers from Latin America, Pablo showed what a good organizer he was.   Millions of
letters had to be sent out.   Pablo was diligent in all matters.
The Congress was a success.   So many people came that it is

impossible to name them all.   It was very moving.   It was
there, in Madrid, that amidst the bombs and the Fascist ad-
vance we saw Miguel Hernández again.   He had come from
the front wearing his militia uniform.   We also met Ilya
Ehrenburg and his wife, who were later to receive us with
great affection in the Soviet Union.   Our house, "the house
of flowers, " as it was called, had been bombed.   Amidst the
ruins, however, our dog Flak appeared.   He had knocked
down a window as he sensed our presence there.   Pablo re-
joiced in seeing him.   As Franco was about to enter the city,
we prepared to return to Chile.   With other Chileans who
were at the Congress, we took a freighter and sailed for
Valparaíso, arriving on the eve of the 1938 presidential elec-
tion.

Pedro Aguirre Cerda was the candidate of the Radical
Party [middle-of-the-road] and the Popular Front [leftist co-
alition dominated by Socialists and Communists.]   Pablo cam-
paigned very actively for Don Pedro and when he won, Pablo
began to put pressures on the new government to open the
doors to Spanish immigration.   After some initial reluctance,
Don Pedro agreed to send Pablo to Paris for the purpose of
organizing the embarkation of Spanish refugees.   Pablo handled
the operation very efficiently and everything was ready for the
ship Winnipeg to sail.   At the last minute, however, Aguirre
Cerda rescinded the embarkation order.   He had given in to
pressures from the Chilean Right--which was opposed to giving refuge to "Communists. "   Pablo was very upset and was
fuming at the ambivalence of his president.   He wired Don
Pedro telling him that if the Winnipeg did not sail he would
shoot himself.   Don Pedro finally consented.   Both the French
and the Chilean governments sent letters of gratitude to Pablo
for the splendid job he had done.   In a personal letter, Don
Pedro thanked Pablo for having sent to Chile so many wonderful Spaniards.

S. B.   Did Pablo resume his diplomatic career under
Pedro Aguirre Cerda?

D. C.   Yes.   Before the death of Don Pedro [in 1941]
Pablo had been named consul-general of Mexico.   It was
there that he met the great muralists.   He had an especially
good relation with David Alfaro Siqueiros--who was in jail at
the time.   Pablo used to visit him and, with the aid of an of-
ficer, used to take him out of jail at night for dinner.   He
secured David a Chilean visa and later was instrumental in
getting him out of the country.   Thanks to Pablo, David Alfaro Siqueiros painted and left many great murals in Chile.

Mexico was not always kind to Pablo. During some poetry recitals there were hostile manifestations against him and against Chile. Once, fearing that there were terrorists in the audience, he had to lecture in a theater with the Mexican police in the wings, holding machine guns.

After the death of Don Pedro Aguirre Cerda in 1941, Pablo renounced his post and we returned to Chile. But our trip took many months. We stopped everywhere. It was on this trip that Pablo visited Machu Picchu for the first time and began writing that monumental poem to its greatness.

Pablo never wrote anything without showing it to me first. He used to say that I was his best critic. Imagine my surprise when he could not write a verse that suited him and asked me to do it. I told him he was crazy. He was the poet, not I.

When we returned to Chile, Pablo became a member of the Communist Party. In 1945 he ran for the Senate and won. A year later, he supported Gabriel González Videla for the presidency, another Radical who was backed by the Popular Front. González Videla won, but was very different from Don Pedro. The new president outlawed the Communist Party and persecuted Pablo--everyone knows this.

S. B.   After González Videla outlawed the Communist Party in 1948 and began his persecution of Pablo Neruda and other prominent Communists, you became fugitives. How did you manage to escape the police and how difficult was life under those circumstances?

D. C.   Life was hectic. We were hiding constantly. Sometimes friends would wake us at three or four in the morning, put us into a car, and drive us to a different town. Once Pablo and I were in a car and a policeman hitched a ride. He sat in the front and we sat in the back. We didn't say a word.

In a sense, that period was very romantic, if you know what I mean. We were able to dodge the police because of the help of so many wonderful people we met. They hid us in their homes, they fed us, they provided us with everything. I remember that we were staying with a family and the children took a liking to us. Especially to Pablo. He would help them build cardboard feeders for hummingbirds. He would tell them to paint the feeders red and put water mixed with

honey in them. The children loved to see the birds feed.
They protected us from strangers. They would not even al-
low relatives to come disturb "Uncle Peter" and "Aunt Sarah."
Those children were wonderful.

Pablo completely outfoxed the Chilean police. He
crossed the border to Argentina. Using a false passport, he
sailed for France. When he arrived, the Chilean police still
thought he was in Chile. The government broadcast that it
was very close to capturing Pablo Neruda. Only a matter of
days now.

I joined Pablo in Paris at a later date, taking his passport with me. Then I returned to Chile to work on behalf of
his legal re-entry into the country. Ex-President Arturo
Alessandri* liked Pablo. Not only because he was a poet and
diplomat, but also because Pablo had been invited to the World
Congress on Peace. This was prestigious for Chile and Don
Arturo intervened, making Pablo's return possible.

S. B. It was around this time that you became separated from Pablo. Would you like to talk about this?

D. C. Pablo and I became legally separated in 1954.
But since 1952 our activities sent us on divergent paths.
Pablo became involved with other people. I became increasingly interested in my art. There was no animosity. There
isn't much more I can say. I loved Pablo and he will always
be in my heart.

S. B. Hormiguita, which of Pablo's books is your favorite?

D. C. I like them all. Perhaps I like the Canto general best, but not because I helped Pablo with its publication.
It is a moving account that narrates the history of America in
epic form. There is no other book of poetry that conveys
with such force the life of our continent and its people.

*   *   *

Our interviews came to an end and I was getting ready

---

*Arturo Alessandri Palma was twice president of Chile, 1920-
1924 and 1932-1938, and throughout his life, wielded consider-
able influence on Chilean politics.

Pablo and Hormiguita. (Courtesy Delia del Carril.)

to leave Chile and return to the United States.   The night before my departure, Hormiguita prepared a farewell dinner for
me and invited her close friends.   As we said good-bye, she
gave me a beautiful edition of the <u>Veinte poemas de amor y</u>
<u>una canción desesperada</u>, illustrated by Mario Toral.   In the
short period of two months we had become very good friends.
Now that I was leaving, I was saddened by the thought that
it might be several years before I could see my friends again.

The conversations I had with Hormiguita revealed a direct, warm-hearted person, who gave of herself unhesitatingly,
and who is much loved by all those who know her.   Her generosity makes clear why.

VIII

PABLO'S DEATH:
CONVERSATIONS WITH MATILDE URRUTIA

This chapter is extracted from an interview with Doña
Matilde Urrutia de Neruda on her husband's death.   The interview came about unexpectedly the day before I left Chile,
and was arranged by a mutual friend, "Queta" (Henriqueta),
wife of Pablo Neruda's photographer and longtime friend, Antonio Quintana Contreras.   Queta and I had met many times
at Delia del Carril's house, and one night Queta suggested
that I get in touch with Matilde.   The interview was set up
and took place on June 19, 1975, in Matilde's home in Santiago.

Houses in Latin America, unlike those in the United
States, are, for the most part, enclosed behind high walls,
each home's wall running into the next, concealing the shapes
of the actual houses within, masking the lives of those
who inhabit them.   Neruda's house, "La Chascona," is
on a small street on the slope of San Cristobal hill, and as
I stood at the doorstep waiting to be let in to see his widow,
I couldn't help but wonder what lay behind the dismal stone
wall, how much had been changed in the reconstruction of this
house which had been destroyed almost in its entirety, during
the first days after the 1973 coup.

I was led from the entrance through a multi-colored
labyrinth of white, yellow, blue and brown walls, up a stair-
way to an open-air patio on the second level, over a small
stream trickling its way through from the hill, and finally,
up a second stair leading into the living room.   Matilde wel-
comed me graciously, though her attitude evinced the with-
drawn air of reserve and mystery I had sensed a few minutes
before on the street.   The bottle of whiskey I had brought her
helped to break the ice; such luxuries are rare in Chile, especially since the change of government.

149

In all, I spent four hours with this perceptive, intelligent but extremely moody woman who, for 21 years, had
been wife, companion, and friend to Latin America's Nobel
Prize winner.   Her initial response to the idea of a taped interview was skeptical, which, given the strict censorship and
political restrictions of Chilean citizens today, is more than
understandable.   Consequently, we spent the first hour becoming better acquainted with one another, discussing my plans
for the book on her husband, and talking about Pablo's literary work.   At one point, I asked her which of his books he
had preferred, and her answer was at first non-committal.
She pointed out that the question had been asked of Pablo
many times, but that he would never answer it since he loved
them all.

Later on, she admitted that among her own favorites
were Estravagario, a personal, happy and humorous book,
and Los versos del capitán, which he had dedicated to her.
At the time he wrote this book, because he was still living
with Delia and did not want to hurt Hormiga, he released it
for publication anonymously.   It was only later on that he admitted being the "captain," thus acknowledging his authorship
of the book.

We discussed her interest in poetry and music, and
her preparation as a singer in the Conservatory of the University of Chile.   We also talked about the beginning of their
relationship, in 1946, when they met at a symphony concert
in the Parque Forestal (in Santiago).   I asked her if she had
any photographs of Pablo at hand.   She shook her head, and
then pointing to her portrait by Diego Rivera, hanging over
the fireplace, she asked whether I could see Pablo.   I looked
at the double profile of her on the wall and had to admit I
could not.   She went up to the fireplace, poked the burning
crackling wood, and pointed to her hair in the painting.   Pablo's face suddenly appeared before my eyes, clearly deline-
ated, expressive, as if to imply that he would always be
present somewhere, everywhere.   She showed me his handwritten poem framed on the wall, and then sat down again and
said, quietly, that she would not answer any questions in any
way related to politics, but she left the subject ambiguously
open, because almost immediately, she added that, if I did

Facing page: Matilde Urrutia in what was Neruda's favorite
chair, at "La Chascona," 1975.   (Photograph by Salvatore
Bizzarro.)

Portrait of Matilde Urrutia, by Diego Rivera, famous Mexican muralist and intimate of the Nerudas. In her hair, on the right, can be seen the profile of Pablo Neruda. (Photograph by Salvatore Bizzarro.)

ask her anything political, she would answer in the way she knew Pablo would have answered.   We settled with ease into our chairs, and the interview began. *

After talking about Neruda's literary work, I asked Doña Matilde how the poet spent his last days, from the September 11th coup to his death on September 23rd.   She answered by saying that this was perhaps the most difficult question posed to her, since neither she, nor anyone else, knew that Pablo was dying.   In fact, just a few days earlier Pablo had received encouraging news from the doctor, who said that because of Pablo's strong will and constitution he had at least six more years to live.

On September 11th, as customary, Pablo and Matilde were on the island (Isla Negra) having an early breakfast. They were listening to the news on the radio, when suddenly it was interrupted by an announcement saying that President Salvador Allende Gossens was going to speak.   They were quite surprised because it was so early.   How could Salvador speak at that hour?   Upon hearing the President's words (by now famous), they were very shocked, remained silent for a long time after, and knew not what to think.   The radio kept broadcasting up-to-the-minute reports and then came all the contradictory decrees which said that no one could leave their homes.   And meanwhile, they felt so far away, so completely alone on the island.

After lunch, they saw the news report on La Moneda on the television.   They watched it three or four times.   Immediately after, Doña Matilde received a telephone call from

---

*An excerpt of this interview, transcribed and translated by Suzanne Oboler, appeared in Folio, a monthly magazine of Pacifica Radio (WBAI) in New York, in their February, 1976, issue.   It was my intention to reproduce the interview verbatim in the present work.   However, after seeing a transcription of the taped interview, Doña Matilde demurred at its inclusion in my book, because the interview touched on certain points which in her opinion were not suitable for a literary study of Pablo Neruda.   The decision to paraphrase our conversation then followed, for it is my belief that what Doña Matilde said is extremely important not only for an understanding of certain aspects of Neruda's final literary production but also for the new light which it sheds on the mystery surrounding his death.   The taped interview is in my possession.

Pablo's doctor advising her to keep the news away from her husband. She pointed out that there was no way of hiding the news from Pablo when at that very moment he was in the bedroom watching the television, and had been listening to the radio all day. The doctor insisted that Doña Matilde make every effort to keep the news away from Pablo or it might be very harmful to his health.

That day, Pablo was very affected by everything going on. Doña Matilde had never seen him like that, but after all, he was sick. That same night, the news reports put him in a very feverish state. Since no one was allowed out of their homes, a nurse couldn't be brought to him to give him an injection. They were completely isolated in Isla Negra, with no medicine, without a doctor, with nothing.

Doña Matilde called the doctor and told him she wanted to bring Pablo to Santiago. He answered that it was impossible: no one could be out on the streets, no car could fetch them, and the roads to Santiago were cut off.

Two or three days after the coup, the junta's emissaries called on them. A great number of military men came, but Doña Matilde knew how to receive them. When she found out that they were coming to search the estate, she asked them where they wanted to begin and told them they were welcome to come and go as they pleased. She took them directly to Pablo's bedroom. It was early in the morning, about ten or ten-thirty, and Pablo was not yet dressed. He was very depressed and very weak, as if someone had given him a terrible blow. He greeted them, offered everyone a drink, and told them to search wherever they pleased, do whatever they had to do, that in any case they were not going to find anything at all in the bedroom.

They were very kind. They didn't want to search the bedroom: they didn't want to disturb him, and actually, their visit to the island was very courteous. They looked around the entire house but they didn't take anything, not even a book. All in all, nothing happened.

She spoke to the doctor again and insisted that she could not take care of Pablo alone any longer, because he was now running a very high fever. He was in a terrible physical state. They had managed to get permission for a nurse to come give him a few injections the doctor had prescribed.

On September 19, she was finally able to get an ambu-
lance to come to take him to Santiago. He was almost dead.
They had to pass through a road block where they were check-
ing all the cars coming from the Island to Santiago. Still in
the car, she told the guards that Pablo Neruda was in the
car, and was very ill. They heard the name, Pablo Neruda,
as if they'd been told it was raining. They ordered her out of
the car and searched it thoroughly, going through the clothes
and blankets, through everything they had in it, looking under-
neath it, everywhere. It was horrible.

When she got back into the car, she was crying. She
always tried to be brave when these things happened, but she
was terribly affected by this. They continued on their way
and finally arrived at the hospital. There, the doctor told
her that Pablo was in a very bad way and that they had to
call a cardiologist. Pablo had never had anything wrong with
him. A few circulation problems, perhaps, but his heart had
always been healthy. The cardiologist came, examined him,
prescribed a few things and left. It was a time when doctors
would run in and out, scared, distraught; they would come,
they would prescribe, they would leave. Matilde and Pablo
were left alone at night with no assistance. It was a terrible time for both since Pablo was in pain and Matilde knew
not what to do. The following morning the Mexican Ambassador, Gonzalo Martínez Corbalá, came to tell Neruda that he
should go to Mexico. The Mexican President, Luis Echever-
ría Alvarez, had invited him personally and was sending a
private plane to fetch him with everything he wanted to bring
with him; whenever he was ready, he could go to Mexico.
Matilde recalls that Pablo was thankful but said no, he would
not leave, he would stay in Chile because he could never live
anywhere else.

On the 21st, Matilde received word that their house in
Santiago had been destroyed and that something could happen
to Pablo. She told her husband about it and advised him that
they should go to Mexico, where they would be safe. She
suggested that they could go for two or three months until order might be restored in Chile, and then return. Pablo was
silent for a long time, about an hour, perhaps two. Matilde
sat there, reading a book--pretending to--though actually, she
was trying to figure out what they should do. Then he said,
"Yes, we'll go. " They called the ambassador and told him
that they would leave. Matilde went to the island to pick up
some clothes, leaving Pablo in care of a boy who had helped
them with some chores. Knowing the condition Pablo was in,

she admonished the boy not to let anyone come see him.   She
had not allowed any of Pablo's friends to come visit so that
they would not tell him what was happening in Chile.   But
while she was away, many of their friends arrived at the hospital, they went into Pablo's room, and began recounting what
was happening in the country.   So, now, they told him everything: that this person had been taken, and such-and-so had
happened to that one...   Doña Matilde's account momentarily
trailed off as she noted that everyone knew what was happening in Chile.   What she had prevented up until that day happened.   Upon her return to the clinic at six o'clock that eve-
ning, she found that Pablo was in a state of madness.   He
was very sick and disturbed.   As the boy told Matilde that
many of Pablo's friends had been in to see him, disregarding
her instructions, Pablo reproached Matilde for having been
with him all along without telling him that the junta was mur-
dering people and that the most atrocious things were happening.   She replied that it was not true, that everything was
being exaggerated, and that one should only believe a part of
what one hears.

That night Matilde was alone with Pablo, and he began
to speak of their honeymoon, of many things which had happened so long ago, things about their years together, and all
of a sudden, she realized that Pablo was saying things that
were not part of his way of being at all; he was saying sweet
things, speaking gently, saying very strange things.   Soon
after, he became delirious and all of his delirium had to do
with what was happening at that moment in Chile.   Worried,
Matilde summoned the nurse and asked her what could be
given to Pablo so that he could sleep comfortably that night.
The nurse left and returned with a sedative and Pablo relaxed
for a while.   But within a short time he became restless, and
Matilde had difficulties in holding him down.   He would escape
her grip and scream; he kept repeating, "they're shooting
them!"

The nurse, who must have heard all this, came back
and gave him another injection.   Little by little, Pablo quieted
down as Matilde very soothingly told him to relax and to try
to sleep.   He finally dozed off, and never woke up again.

He slept all that night, and the following day was still
breathing in what Matilde described as a difficult sleep.   At
times he was delirious, but never recovered consciousness.
Then, on the night of the 23rd, at 10:30, he passed from
sleep into death.   He never suffered physically, Matilde said.

The first moments were horrible for Doña Matilde.
She was with a friend and one of Pablo's sisters, who had
come to spend the night as news that Pablo was very ill
reached her.   That same night, the hospital staff instructed
Matilde that she had to dress Pablo.   She suggested that
they wait until morning.   She knew so very little about death;
she didn't know the dead had to be dressed immediately.   She
had never had any contact with a dying man before.   So, she
had to come out of that state of shock and anguish which had
left her so numb, from that terrible feeling she had, and help
dress her husband.   Matilde and Pablo's sister and the other
friend got Pablo dressed.   Then the nurse came in to help
them with further instructions, and an orderly appeared.   The
latter removed Pablo from the bed and placed him in a rolling
bed, racing the body down the corridors.   To Matilde, all
this seemed so macabre.

Suddenly, the orderly, the nurse and Neruda's body
disappeared into an enormous elevator.   Doña Matilde managed
to slip in just as its doors were closing.   She asked where
they were taking Pablo, and they answered that he had to be
taken downstairs.   She wanted to know what was downstairs,
but they did not answer her.   As they left the elevator, she
lost them in the hallway, but found them again, just as they
were abandoning her husband's body in a dark corridor through
which a freezing night wind gusted continuously.   They warned
her that she was not allowed to remain there, and she told
them emphatically that she was not going to be separated from
her husband, that she would not leave him then, nor at any
moment.   When they insisted that she leave, she retorted that
she would remain, that neither they, nor anyone else, could
prevent her from staying with Pablo.

Doña Matilde recalls that she must have looked like a
mad woman; she was completely out of control.   She asked in-
sistently that they bring her a chair.   They finally agreed,
seeing that they could not move her, and she stayed there with
Pablo all night, the wind sweeping through the hallway.   By
the time the newspaper reporters came the next morning, she
was frozen.   She was numb all over her body and could not
feel her hands and feet.

The reporters arrived about eight o'clock--no one was
allowed into the hospital before then--and, as soon as they
arrived, Pablo was taken into a waiting room (lounge) so that
he could be seen, so that the press had a nice room to go to.
Doña Matilde was upset by this, and seeing the same people of

the hospital who had treated her so inhumanely the night before she asked them why could they have not brought the ca-
daver to the lounge instead of leaving her crying in that frozen hallway. Such, for Doña Matilde, are the inhuman aspects of death, which have to be lived, experienced, to know
that they exist.

When the newspapermen arrived, many of the Neruda's
friends came too. They asked Matilde where she was going
to take Pablo and she replied that she would take him to their
house in Santiago. Then they told her what she already knew,
that their house had been destroyed, and that there would be
not one room in which to mourn him. Since the house was
so enormous, and had so many wings and so many rooms,
she was sure that one of them had to be in good-enough condition for them to be able to take Pablo there. But when she
finally went to see the house, she found that the soldiers had
destroyed practically everything (it was assumed that it was
done by soldiers of the junta although it was never ascer-
tained). They had not left anything undamaged, and those
things which had not been torn down, had been made
worthless. The canal which runs through the entrance hall
had flooded the entire house, a little footbridge across it had
been destroyed, and the water had risen about eighty centi-
meters. In order to bring Pablo into the house, Matilde and
her friends had to build a new bridge across the canal.

Doña Matilde didn't quite know what to do. But by the
time she reached the house with her husband's body, all the
neighbors had come to see what was going on. She asked
them to help her by bringing things, old things, anything they
didn't want to fill-in the canal. They all began to bring whatever they could find which could be useful, and, at last, the
canal was filled. Miraculously, they had made a bridge from
sticks, boards, wood, and were able to carry Pablo across
into the house.

I asked Doña Matilde whether, after the wake, Pablo
was allowed to be buried where he would have liked to be,
and whether or not he had expressed any wishes about a particular place. She thought for a moment, and a painful expression marked her serene face, then she answered that he
had been denied burial to the very day of this conversation,
and that this represented her greatest burden. Pablo had indeed chosen a place. He had left in writing, everywhere,
that he wanted to be buried on the island. There is a small
hill there, away from the house and from everything; there is

a path going up to it.   She and Pablo always thought that they
would be able to get permission for him to be buried on the
hill.   The new government, however, denied Matilde permission.   As a result, Pablo was presently in a temporary niche,
a peasant's niche, just an ordinary one.   At some future
time, he would have to be taken from there.   For a short
time, immediately after his death, he was placed in a family
graveyard, a wealthy family by the name of Disborn, at the
insistence of their daughter, a Disborn who loved Pablo's
poetry and his political commitment.   Several of the woman's
relatives, however, objected to his being there, so he had to
be moved.   Doña Matilde had to take him from there at the
last moment and the quickest thing was to buy him a niche in
the Santiago cemetery.

Referring to her husband's humble grave, Doña Matilde
said that many people visit him.   They are always there; he
always has flowers.   Whenever Doña Matilde has been away
from Chile she always rushes back to the cemetery when she
returns, thinking that Pablo's grave might have been neglected
and without flowers.   But no, he has flowers always, and
people write many messages for him on the marble tombstone.
Of course, the people who work in the cemetery have been ordered to erase anything that is written to him; but even if
they do, new messages appear with fresh flowers, gestures of
people who love him and call him Pablo, friend.

From our discussion of Pablo's death and his subsequent burial, Doña Matilde and I shifted our concerns to literary problems.   I reminded Doña Matilde that Pablo Neruda,
at the end of his Memoirs, had written three pages about Allende's murder, which were apparently finished on September
14th.   I asked her about the allegation that those three pages
had not been written by Pablo Neruda, but by a Venezuelan
author, Miguel Otero Silva.   She replied that such a claim
was a show of absolute ignorance about herself, about Miguel
Otero and about Pablo.   There is not one student of Pablo's
work, she continued, who would state, or even insinuate,
something of the sort.   That was a rumor begun in Chile.
She, herself, as Pablo's wife, who now lives for his memory
and for the many things which still remain to be done in
terms of what Pablo has left behind, would never allow one
word to be added, not even a syllable, to his work.   Nor
would Miguel, a man who had been almost a brother to Pablo,
and who had enormous respect for him.   When he was writing
the Memoirs, Pablo was dictating them, and when anything is
dictated there are always going to be words repeated.   Matilde

said that when she and Miguel Otero were editing the Memoirs, whenever a word had to be changed, the Venezuelan
would always look for a word Pablo would use, a word he
had used.

To illustrate this further, she went on telling me that
when she was in Paris she had talked to Robert Pring-Mill,
a British scholar from Oxford and a connoisseur of Neruda's
works. She had asked him the same question I had just put
to her, regarding the authenticity of the last three pages of
the Memoirs. His answer was that nobody who had studied
Pablo's work would ever say that, principally because Pablo's
prose is unique; no other prose like Neruda's exists. His
prose is so original that no one could imitate it. (If perchance
someone else had written that chapter, Pring-Mill told Matilde, that would mean that that man is a marvelous writer, and
should continue to write. But in fact no one could imitate
Pablo.)

Doña Matilde pointed out, finally, that she would lose
all the serenity in her life, had she added or deleted anything.
And furthermore, at that time, it had been dangerous for her
to include that chapter, she had run a risk by doing it. I
asked her whether she had, then, taken the original manuscript
to the publisher ready to be transcribed. She answered affir-
matively, noting that she was the only person who, with absolute certainty, knew everything, and had all the material. In
her opinion such questions were therefore to be asked of the
students, and scholars, since they are the people who study
Pablo's work. As for Pablo himself, he had to write something and the people who knew him knew that he couldn't have
ignored and not written about such an important moment in
history, such fundamental developments. How could Pablo not
have written about them?

I pointed out that I had been told in Chile over and
over, including by herself, that on September 14, Pablo was
very sick, and that perhaps he would not have been capable of
writing at all, being as sick as he was, and with a fever.

She answered that Pablo wrote in the clinic. The day
before he lost consciousness he was working all morning, with
his secretary, Homero Arce, finishing off his books of poems,
because, as he and Doña Matilde were going away to Mexico,
he wanted to leave everything with his editor. So he finished
everything off. All his books published posthumously were in
fact arranged and structured by him.

Doña Matilde added that from the 11th to the 14th,
three days of great tension elapsed, during which the two of
them had been alone on the island, and during which he could
have dictated much of it.   How, she wondered, could people
be so sure he hadn't? She was convinced it was a deliberately launched fabrication--one, however, that could never be believed by anyone who knew Pablo's work, and who knew her,
or Miguel.   Her respect for what Pablo left was too great.
She noted also that sometimes people would ask her questions
deliberately to see what she said or to see if she would exag-
gerate ... but she never exaggerated anything.   For example
they said that Isla Negra was destroyed, that Pablo's library
was destroyed. She had always said that that was not true.
Pablo's library couldn't have been destroyed because it was
on a boat, on its way from France.   Pablo had taken most of
his library to France, so it was still on a ship, on its way
back to Chile.

Since she had mentioned France, I asked her about
Pablo Neruda's stay there as Chilean ambassador during the
Allende government.   I was particularly interested in why he
had resigned from his post and returned to Chile after a year
and ten months in Paris.   There were rumors that Pablo had
returned because his health was failing.

Doña Matilde was glad to be able to talk about that
too, since many things had been said about that which in her
view were not true.   Pablo had decided to return to Chile because he had been awarded the Nobel Prize in 1971 and people
were anxious to congratulate him, to welcome him back.   He
had decided on November 10th as the day he would return
home.   And in Chile they had prepared a big reception for
him in the National Stadium, and everyone was coming to hear
Pablo.   He was also returning home with two months' vaca-
tion time due him.   She added that he was very anxious to return to the island and to see the ocean.

When Doña Matilde and Pablo arrived in Chile, Salvador Allende was in the United States, attending a meeting of
the United Nations in New York, so they were met by General
Carlos Prats González,* who received Pablo at the National

---

*Army chief of staff under Allende; murdered in Buenos Aires
in September, 1974, one of many said to have been on the
Junta's "hate list"; strong evidence affixes responsibility for
his death on the National Intelligence Directorate (DINA), the
Chilean secret police (disbanded since August 1977).

Stadium and gave a beautiful welcoming speech, being after all, a very cultured and intelligent man.

After the ceremonies in Santiago, Pablo and Matilde went to Isla Negra and, as soon as they arrived on the island, Pablo opened the bedroom windows from which one can see far across the ocean, and all the rocks; San Antonio, a small fishing village and port can be seen too.   On the opposite side is Isla Negra, * where the birds and the ocean waves strike the shore; it's a marvelous spectacle which one can't help but feel.

Seeing the magnificent landscape, Pablo had turned to Matilde saying "What am I doing in Paris?" He pledged never to return to France, since life in Chile was so wonderful.   What more did he need?   At that very moment, he had picked up the phone and called Salvador Allende in New York. Pablo was lucky to be able to reach him immediately, and told the President he was never going back to his ambassadorial post.   Allende laughed a lot and told his most famous poet that he was always free to do what he wanted.   Pablo thought that his friend Salvador had received the news as if it was in jest.   But Pablo had, in fact, given him his resignation, over the telephone, long distance.

At this point I interrupted Doña Matilde's account, noting that many people claimed that Pablo had resigned because of illness; that he was anemic and suffering from cancer. She replied that Pablo had been anemic since birth and that his cancer was in the initial state, and that he had never suffered any pain because of it.   This was something which consoled her to a certain extent.

Pablo had not suffered because his cancer did not have a chance to develop, although that could have happened from one moment to the next.   It was cancer of the prostate and, of course, as it develops, it grows and spreads.   However, this is one of the slowest types of cancer, and five or six years can go by before it becomes fatal.   Life had freed him from suffering--or rather, not life, but death had.

I went back to the problem of authorship, referring to

---

*The Nerudas called their house, located on the Chilean coast near Valparaíso, "Isla Negra" even though the island itself is on the opposite side.

another poem of which it is also said that Pablo was not the
author. It was written when the President of the United
States, Richard M. Nixon, decided to bomb North Vietnam
and to mine the port of Haiphong. It had Neruda's signature,
but some of his detractors in Chile had said that he could
not have written it. The long poem appeared in a booklet
entitled, Nixonicidio and the Chilean Revolution (Nixonicidio
y la revolución chilena). I asked Doña Matilde what she
could say about this. She responded that there was very little
she could say about it. Pablo had written the booklet in a
week upon his return to Chile. Since the Chilean congressional elections were at that time, he wanted to publish it for the
occasion. Naturally, everything that was happening in Vietnam affected him a great deal. And, logically, since Nixon
was the President of the United States, he was to blame for
what was happening in Vietnam because he could have prevented it. So Pablo had written the poem, which was a call
to all writers to come together and kill Nixon. But he wished
to kill him with sonnets, which makes for a very strange
murder. He wanted to kill Nixon with poetry.

Doña Matilde had never heard it said that Pablo had
not written it. I had to confess that it was a rumor I had
heard in Chile from somewhat unreliable sources, and she
noted that the poem had appeared long before Pablo's death
and prior to the March, 1973, congressional elections.

To put aside further doubt, Doña Matilde added that
Pablo's poetry books, the originals, were all handwritten, so
that no one could say he had not written them. All his
poems were scribbled by hand; only the prose had been dictated.

I asked Doña Matilde how she now spent her time, after the terrible shock which Pablo Neruda's death had caused
her, since he was the one person to whom her whole life had
been dedicated. She answered that, since Pablo had kept her
always occupied, she was busy even after his death. There
was so much to do and she lived for his memory. For example, the entire preceding year had been spent reconstructing
their house in Santiago.

I inquired if the house looked then as it had before it
was destroyed and vandalized, and she said that it was just
like it, although a small section was different because it was
difficult to make everything look as it was.

Later we talked about other things that kept Neruda's widow occupied, and among the most important she mentioned having to rearrange her husband's library, which at the time of his death was being shipped from France.   Since the library was on the island, it had to be well-protected because the books suffered a great deal on account of the humidity.   She often made trips to Isla Negra to see how the books fared, and to work on other things which Pablo had left behind: preserving, arranging, and fixing everything.

Before his death, Pablo Neruda had willed his house in Isla Negra to the Communist Party.   As a result, the Chilean Junta had expropriated it and Doña Matilde was being kept busy convincing the government that the house should be turned into a museum.

As the interview drew to a close, I asked Doña Matilde if she ever planned to leave Chile forever someday.   Her answer was an emphatic no.   She would leave for two or three months at a time, but she would always return.   She was born in Chile and she could not live anywhere else.   She would always be at Pablo's side.

Chronologically, the death of Pablo Neruda almost coincided with the death of Salvador Allende.   Like Allende, Neruda will inevitably become a symbol for the death of Chile.

Conclusion to Part II

When in October, 1971, the Secretary General of the
Swedish Academy, Karl Ragner Gierow, awarded the Nobel
Prize in Literature to Ricardo Eliezer Neftalí Reyes y Basoalto, some of the audience must have wondered what obscure writer the academy had chosen. But when after a the-
atrical pause Gierow added, "Also known as Pablo Neruda,"
the puzzled expressions disappeared.

Today, Pablo Neruda is the best known Latin American
poet. The birth of the American continent, the rains of his
native Parral, the arid north, Machu Picchu and the Cordillera de los Andes, the ocean beating on the Chilean coast,
the earthquakes, the flowers, the trees and the birds, are all
part of the lushness of language and images that recreate his
natural world. Whether he is evoking his father's beard or
a dead carob tree, he is a writer who offers a hymn in worship of what he sees, and has an ear unmatched among his
contemporaries for the off-rhythms that can be made to rattle
in the sonorities of a line of blank verse.

Neruda is difficult to characterize because he is more
complex and private than most of his fellow poets. In spite
of this, his poetic development is easy to follow: we have the
love poetry written during his twenties; the poetry of death
and introspection, written in his thirties; the epic poetry and
the poetry of solidarity, written in his forties; the poetry that
strips down both manner and matter as he glorifies every object he observes, written in his fifties; and the later poetry,
which is more personal and autobiographical and leads to his
last work, the Memoirs.

At first, we have a hermetic poet with a rather desolate vision of the world born of an inability to fathom the
meaning of man's destiny and to achieve harmony with the surrounding reality. It is a poetry of spiritual unrest, most attentive to suffering and to the harshness of an absurd existence. Sometimes arcane, it expresses the poet's own private concerns: grievances over the absence of love, the mo-
notony of the days that bear no fruit, the omnipresence of

165

insignificant death, and the need to experience and utter
something meaningful.

It was the Spanish Civil War that provided Neruda with
the experience necessary to express fully his poetic soul.
The inhumanity of war shocked him out of his private anguish
and he became profoundly conscious of his fellow human beings.

Political persecution and exile make Neruda evoke the
Chilean environment, with its parched and stony beaches and
reef-strewn stretches of sea. He became nostalgic and his
pages fill with love for the sea, water and rain of the south.
In his verse, we can also feel the yearning for the purity of
lost youth and the idyllic beauty of a homeland beyond reach.

With the Odes, Neruda greatly simplifies his style,
seeking understanding from his most humble readers.   Later
books of poems, more personal and narrative in nature than
the Odes, are rendering of intensely experienced moments
spent in the company of the beloved woman, or in the contemplation of the self.

These times of introspection, frustrated love, war,
famine, exile, happiness, betrayal, suffering have been his
times and, with his love for people and nature, have formed
the background of his poetry. From Crepusculario to Estravagario, from the Memorial de Isla Negra to the Memoirs,
we go through more than fifty years of poetic creation. The
road is long, at times difficult, but the poet gives a splendid
journey, never lacking in warmth, compassion and humanity.

In the scrupulously edited pages of his work, the poet
has made his life intimately known to the reader. Ultimate-
ly, to judge his poetry is to judge his integrity as well as
the scope of his understanding. In our analysis we have discovered that it is impossible to separate the writer from his
subject, and the poems have only one real subject: Pablo
Neruda.

CHAPTER NOTES

INTRODUCTION

[1] Pablo Neruda, Obras completas, 2d ed. (Buenos Aires: Editorial Losada, 1962), p648. A third edition of the Obras completas appeared in two volumes in 1968, and a fourth edition appeared in three volumes in 1973. Both were published by Losada.

[2] Arthur Lundkvist, "Neruda," Boletín no. 45 (diciembre 1963), 50.

[3] Pablo Neruda, Memorias: Confieso que he vivido, 2d ed. (Buenos Aires: Editorial Losada, 1974), p18: "Era diligente y dulce, tenía sentido de humor campesino, una bondad activa e infatigable."

[4] Jaime Alazraki, Poética y poesía de Pablo Neruda (New York: Las Américas Pub. Co., 1965), p55.

[5] Lundkvist, "Neruda," 50.

[6] Margarita Aguirre, Genio y figura de Pablo Neruda (Buenos Aires: Editorial Universitaria, 1964), p66.

[7] E. Rodríguez Monegal, El viajero inmóvil (Buenos Aires: Editorial Losada, 1966), pp31-2.

[8] Pedro Henríquez Ureña, Las corrientes literarias en Hispano-américa (México: Fondo de Cultura Económica, 1949), p185.

[9] Concha Meléndez, "Pablo Neruda en su extremo imperio," Revista Hispánica Moderna II (1936), 12.

[10] Because of the outbreak of the Spanish Civil War, only six issues were published and the review was discontinued.

In it, Neruda rejected the "arte puro" and the "arte deshumanizado" in favor of a more subjective poetry.

[11] Lundkvist, "Neruda, " 55.

[12] Rodríguez Monegal, El viajero, pp181-228.

[13] For a discussion of the chaotic enumeration in modern poetry see Leo Spitzer, La enumeración caótica en la poesía moderna (Buenos Aires: Facultad de Filosofía y Letras, 1945).

CHAPTER I

[1] See, for example, Amado Alonso, Poesía y estilo de Pablo Neruda, 4th ed. (Buenos Aires: Editorial Sudamericana, 1968), pp348-54; Rodríguez Monegal, El viajero, pp. 228-31; Mario Rodríguez Fernández, "Reunión bajo las nuevas banderas o de la conversión poética de Pablo Neruda, " Mapocho II, no. 3 (1964), 238-48; and Lundkvist, "Neruda, " 49-66.

[2] Alfredo Cardona Peña, Pablo Neruda y otros ensayos (México: Ediciones de Andrea, 1955), p32.

[3] In spite of his public repudiation of the poems of Residencia en la tierra I and II, Neruda continued to allow their publication the rest of his life.

[4] Pablo Neruda; Pedro Pomar and Jorge Amado, O partido comunista e a libertade da criação (Rio de Janeiro: Ediçōes Horizonte, 1946), p8.

[5] Ibid.

[6] Ibid.

[7] Diego Muñoz, "Pablo Neruda: vida y poesía, " Mapocho II, no. 3 (1964), 193.

[8] Rodríguez Fernández, "Reunión, " 244.

[9] Ibid. , 240.

[10] For a discussion of the language of introspection and proclamation in lyrical poetry, see Wolfgang Kayser, Interpretación y análisis de la obra literaria (Madrid: Editorial Gredos, 1961), pp437-53.

[11]Fernando Alegría, "La evolución poética de Pablo Neruda," El libro y el pueblo (México) XIX, no. 30 (1957), 34-5.

CHAPTER II

[1]Rodríguez Monegal, El viajero, p93.

[2]Pablo Neruda, España en el corazón (Ejército del Este: Ediciones Literarias del Comisariado, 1938).

[3]Raúl Morales Alvárez, "El arte de mañana será un quemante reportaje hecho de la actualidad," Ercilla III, no. 132 (1937), 32.

[4]Bernard Gicovate, "Dos Notas sobre poesía y política," Ensayos sobre poesía hispánica (México: Colección Studium--59, 1967), p114.

[5]For an analysis of Neruda's poetic evolution see Alazraki, Poética y poesía, pp61-167.

[6]Rodríguez Monegal, El viajero, p223.

[7]Jaime Alazraki had already noted the similarities between Darío and Neruda in the verses we cite, in Poética y poesía, pp17-8.

[8]Rubén Darío, Cantos de vida y esperanza (Madrid: Espasa-Calpe, 1964), p126.

[9]Ibid., p25.

[10]Alazraki, Poética y poesía, p194.

CHAPTER III

[1]Pablo Neruda, Obras completas, 2d ed. (1962), p12.

[2]Rodríguez Monegal, El viajero, p236.

[3]Giuseppe Bellini, Pablo Neruda (Milan: Nuova Accademia Editrice, 1960), p34.

[4]Cardona Peña, Pablo Neruda, p49.

[5]See the works of Giuseppe Bellini, E. Rodríguez Monegal, and Arthur Lundkvist, cited above.

[6]Rodríguez Monegal, El viajero, p248.

[7]John H. R. Polt, "Elementos gongorinos en 'El gran océano' de Pablo Neruda, " Revista Hispánica Moderna I (1961), 22-31.

CHAPTER IV

[1]Machu Picchu was rediscovered, after nearly four centuries of abandon, by the American explorer Hiram Bingham in 1911, following three earlier unsuccessful expeditions which had begun in 1906. See his book, Lost City of the Incas, 3d ed. (New York: Duell, Sloan, and Pearce, 1948).

[2]In an interview I had with the poet in his house in Isla Negra, on December 22, 1968, Neruda emphasized the connection between events that touched his life in 1945 and his composition of "Alturas de Machu Picchu, " which indicate a definite political orientation in his work.

[3]The interested reader should turn to Nathaniel Tarn's delightful translation of Alturas de Machu Picchu in its entirety. See note 4.

[4]Pablo Neruda, The Heights of Macchu Picchu, translated by Nathaniel Tarn with a Preface by Robert Pring-Mill (London: Jonathan Cape, 1966), p11.

[5]Ibid.

CONCLUSION to Part I

[1]Federico de Onís, Antología de la poesía española e hispanoamericana (New York: Las Américas Pub. Co., 1961), pp29-30.

CHAPTER V

[1]Pablo Neruda, The Elementary Odes, translated by Carlos Lozano with an Introduction by Fernando Alegría (New York: Las Américas Pub. Co., 1961), p17.

[2] Ibid.

[3] Walt Whitman, Leaves of Grass (Modern Library) (New York: Random House, 1950), p23.

[4] Rodríguez Monegal, El viajero, pp268-80.

[5] Pablo Neruda, Extravagaria, translated by Alastair Reid (New York: Noonday Press, 1974).

[6] Rodríguez Monegal, El viajero, p291.

[7] Translation by Alastair Reid (see note 5), Extravagaria, p17.

[8] Ibid., p297.

[9] Ibid., p299.

[10] Ibid., pp99-101.

[11] Ibid., p299.

[12] Rodríguez Monegal, El viajero, p303.

[13] Ibid., p321.

[14] Pablo Neruda, Obras completas, 4th ed. (Buenos Aires: Editorial Losada, 1973; 3 vols.), v2, p1027.

[15] Luis F. González-Cruz, Pablo Neruda y el Memorial de Isla Negra (Miami: Ediciones Universal, 1972), p101. Both González-Cruz and Rodríguez Monegal have pointed out that the poems to Josie Bliss belong chronologically to the second volume and those to Delia del Carril, the third.

[16] Rodríguez Monegal, El viajero, p303.

CHAPTER VI

[1] Pablo Neruda, Memorias: confieso que he vivido, p7. For an excellent translation of this work, see Pablo Neruda, Memoirs, translated by Hardy St. Martin (New York: Farrar, Straus & Giroux, 1977).

[2] The Christian Science Monitor, "Neruda's Memoirs Disclose an Irresistible Storyteller," March 8, 1977, 26.

[3]As quoted in <u>Time</u>, "Prize for a Chilean Poet," November 1, 1971, 47.

[4]<u>Christian Science Monitor</u>, "Neruda's Memoirs," 26.

[5]<u>Ibid.</u>

[6]<u>Ibid.</u>

[7]<u>Time</u>, "Prize," 48.

[8]Jorge Edwards, "The Posthumous Fate of Pablo Neruda," <u>The Times Literary Supplement</u> (London), August 6, 1976, "Latin America," 3-4).

BIBLIOGRAPHY

WORKS BY NERUDA

La canción de la fiesta / Song of Merriment   1921

Crepusculario / Crepusculario   1923

Veinte poemas de amor y una canción desesperada / Twenty
    Love Poems and a Song of Despair   1924

Tentativa del hombre infinito / Trial of the Infinite Man   1926

El habitante y su esperanza / The Inhabitant and His Hope
    1926

Anillos / Rings   1926

El hondero entusiasta / The Fervorous Slinger   1933

Residencia en la tierra I and II / Residence on Earth I and II
    1925-31, 1931-35

España en el corazón / Spain in My Heart   1938

Tercera residencia / The Third Residence   1947

Canto general / Canto general   1950

Los versos del capitán / The Captain's Verses   1952

Poesía política / Political poetry   1953

Las uvas y el viento / The Grapes and the Wind   1954

Odas elementales / Elemental Odes   1954

Viajes / Journeys   1955

Nuevas odas elementales / New Elemental Odes   1956

Tercer libro de odas / The Third Book of Odes   1957

Obras completas / Complete Works   1957

Estravagario / Extravagaria   1958

Navegaciones y regresos / Sea Voyages and Homecomings
    1959

Cien sonetos de amor / One Hundred Sonnets of Love   1959

Canción de gesta / Epic Song (Chanson de geste)   1960

Las piedras de Chile / The Stones of Chile   1961

Cantos ceremoniales / Ceremonial Songs   1961

Plenos poderes / Full Powers   1962

Discursos con Nicanor Parra / Conversations with Nicanor Parra   1962

Obras completas (2d ed.) / Complete Works   1962

Memorial de Isla Negra / Notes from Isla Negra   1963

Arte de pájaros / The Art of Birds   1966

Una casa en la arena / The Beach House   1966

La Barcarola / Barcarole   1967

Fulgor y muerte de Joaquín Murieta / Splendor and Death of Joaquin Murieta   1967

Las manos del dia / The Hands of Day   1968

Obras completas (3d ed.) / Complete Works   1968

Comiendo en Hungría / Eating in Hungary   1969

Aún / Still   1969

Fin de mundo / End of the World   1969

La espada encendida / The Flaming Sword   1970

Las piedras del cielo / The Heavenly Stones   1970

Geografía infructuosa / Barren Earth   1972

La rosa separada / A Rose Apart   1972

Incitación al Nixonicidio y alabanza de la Revolución chilena / A Call for Nixonicide and Praise for the Chilean Revolution   1973

El mar y las campanas / The Sea and the Bells   1973

2000 / 2000   1973

Jardín de invierno / Winter Garden   1973

Obras completas (4th ed.) Complete Works   1973

El corazón amarillo / The Yellow Heart   1974

Libro de las preguntas / The Book of Riddles   1974

Elegía / Elegy   1974

Defectos escogidos / Selected Defects   1974

Confieso que he vivido: Memorias / Memoirs   1974

WORKS ON NERUDA

BIBLIOGRAPHIES

Escudero, Alfonso M. "Fuentes para el conocimiento de Neruda," Mapocho (Santiago) II, no. 3 (1964).

Loyola, Hernán. "Summa bibliográfica de la obra nerudiana," Mapocho (Santiago) III, no. 3 (1965).

Rosembaum, Sidonia. "Pablo Neruda: bibliografía," Revista Hispánica Moderna (New York) XI (1936).

Sanhueza, Jorge. "Bibliografía de Pablo Neruda," in Obras completas, 4th rev. ed. Buenos Aires: Editorial Losada, 1973.

BOOKS AND ARTICLES

Aguirre, Margarita. Genio y figura de Pablo Neruda. Buenos Aires: Editorial Universitaria (EUDEBA), 1964.

Alazraki, Jaime. Poética y poesía de Pablo Neruda. New York: Las Américas Pub. Co., 1965.

Aldunate Philips, Arturo. El nuevo arte poético y Pablo Neruda. Santiago: Editorial Nascimento, 1936.

Alegría, Fernando. "La evolución poética de Pablo Neruda," El Libro y el Pueblo (México) XIX, no. 30 (1957).

_____. "Pablo Neruda," The Berkeley Review I, no. 2 (1957).

Allende, Tomás. "El mensage de Pablo Neruda," La Prensa (Lima), August 22, 1943.

Alonso, Amado. Poesía y estilo de Pablo Neruda: interpretación de una poesía hermética. Buenos Aires: Editorial Losada, 1940. (2d rev. ed. Buenos Aires: Editorial Sudamericana, 1951; 3d ed., Sudamericana, 1966; 4th ed., Sudamericana, 1968.)

Arriaza, Alfredo A. "Grandes poetas de América: Pablo
   Neruda, " Simiente (El Salvador) no. 4 (1946).

Bellini, Giuseppe. Pablo Neruda. Milan: Nuova Accademia
   Editrice, 1960.

Blanco-Fombona, Rufino. "Pablo Neruda, " The South American Journal (London) CXLV, no. 18 (1948).

Cardona Peña, Alfredo. "Lectura de Pablo Neruda, " El Nacional (Mexico), June 25, 1950.

_____. Pablo Neruda y otros ensayos. México: Colec-
   ción Studium-7, 1955.

Chávez, Fermín. "Neruda y su canto epico americano, "
   Capricornia (Buenos Aires), July 1954.

Concha, Jaime. "Cantos ceremoniales, " Mapocho (Santiago)
   I, no. 3 (1963).

_____. "Interpretación de Residencia en la tierra, " Ma-
   pocho (Santiago) II, no. 2 (1963).

Cruchaga, Angel Santa María. "España en el corazón de Pablo Neruda es una obra de pólvora, sollozo y angustia, "
   Ercilla (Santiago) III, no. 139 (1937).

Delano, Luis Enrique. "Metamórfosis de Pablo Neruda, " Aurora de Chile (Santiago) IV, no. 11 (1939).

_____. "Pablo Neruda: Poet in Arms, " Mainstream (New
   York), fall 1947.

Ehrenburg, Ilya. "Introducción, " in Pablo Neruda, 'Poesía
   política. Santiago: Editorial Austral, 1953.

Flores, Angel (ed.). Aproximaciones a Pablo Neruda. Barcelona: Colección Ocnos, 1974.

Felebo. "En torno a Neruda, " Mapocho (Santiago) II, no. 3
   (1964).

Facio, Sara, and Alicia D'Amico. Geografía de Pablo Neruda. Barcelona: Ayma, 1973.

Gallina, A. M. "Poesía de Pablo Neruda" (Translated into

Spanish by Salvatore Quasimodo), Quaderni Ibero-Americani (Turin) no. 16 (1954).

Gicovate, Bernard. "Dos notas sobre poesía y política," Ensayos sobre poesía hispánica. México: Colección Studium-59, 1967.

Giordano, Jaime. "Introducción al Canto General," Mapocho (Santiago) II, no. 3 (1964).

Gonzalez Cruz, Luis F. Pablo Neruda y el Memorial de Isla Negra. Miami: Ediciones Universal, 1972.

Gonzalez Tuñon, Raúl. "España en el corazón," Literatura (Havana) no. 2 (1938).

Guillén, Nicolás. "Evocación de Pablo Neruda," El Espectador (Bogotá), April 3, 1949.

_____. "Pablo Neruda en la Habana," Iloy (Havana), July 3, 1950.

Lellis, Mario Jorge de. Pablo Neruda. Buenos Aires: La Mandragora, 1959.

Lipschutz. "Alturas de Machu Picchu, visión indiana americana," Repertorio Americano, November 10, 1949.

Lowenfels, Walter, ed. For Neruda, for Chile. Boston: Beacon Press, 1974.

Loyola, Hernán. Ser y morir en Pablo Neruda. Santiago: Editora Santiago, 1967.

Lundkvist, Arthur. "Neruda," Boletín (Santiago, Universidad de Chile) no. 45 (December 1963).

Manauta, Juan José. "Canto general, culminación del tema del hombre en la poesía de Pablo Neruda," Cuadernos de Cultura (Buenos Aires), October 1952.

Mancisidor, José. "Neruda en su Canto general," El Nacional (México), September 11, 1950.

Masiukevich, V. "Pablo Neruda, cantor de la paz y de la democracia," Bulletin de l'Académie des Sciences de l'U.R.S.S. (Moscow) no. 27 (1951).

Meléndez, Concha.   "España en el corazón de Pablo Neruda,"
Repertorio Americano, September 14, 1950.

_____. "Pablo Neruda en su extremo imperio," Revista
Hispánica Moderna II (1936).

_____. "Tercera residencia de Pablo Neruda," Asonante
(San Juan de Puerto Rico) VI, no. 2 (1950).

Meo Zilio, J. "Influencia de Sabat Ercasty en Pablo Neruda,"
Revista Nacional (Montevideo) IV, no. 202 (1956).

Montes, Hugo.   "Acerca de Alturas de Machu Picchu," Mapocho (Santiago) II, no. 3 (1964).

_____. La lírica chilena de hoy.   Santiago: Zig-Zag,
1967.

Murena, H. A. "A propósito del Canto general," Sur (Buenos
Aires) no. 198 (1951).

Osses, Mario.   Trinidad poética de Chile: Angel Cruchaga
Santa Maria, Gabriela Mistral y Pablo Neruda.   Santiago:
Universidad de Chile, 1947.

"Pablo Neruda a los 65 años," Enfoque (Santiago) no. 31 (1969).

Paseyro, Ricardo.   "El mito de Neruda," Cuadernos del Congreso por la Libertad de la Cultura (Paris) no. 30 (1958).

_____; Arturo Torres Ríoseco and Juan Ramón Jiménez.
Mito y verdad de Pablo Neruda.   México: Asociación
Mexicana para la Libertad de la Cultura, 1958.

Paz, Octavio. "Pablo Neruda en el corazón," Ruta (México)
no. 4 (1938).

Pérez Galo, René.   Cinco rostros de la poesía.   Quito: Editorial universitaria, 1960.

Polt, John H. R.   "Elementos gongorinos en 'El gran océano'
de Pablo Neruda," Revista Hispánica Moderna (New York)
XVII (1961).

Prado, Rodríguez. "Que despierte el leñador," España Libre
(New York) November 26, 1948.

"El recluso de Isla Negra," Ercilla (Santiago) no. 1777 (1969).

Rivas, Mario. "Exégesis del poema 'Alturas de Machu Picchu.'" Santiago: Imprenta y Litografía Stanley, 1955.

Rodríguez, Fernández Mario. "Reunión bajo las nuevas banderas o de la conversión poética de Pablo Neruda," Mapocho (Santiago) II, no. 3 (1964).

Rodríguez Monegal, E. "Con Pablo Neruda en Montevideo; Politicos, poetas y bibliófilos," Marcha (Montevideo), August 15, 1952.

_____. "Exégesis del poema 'Alturas de Machu Picchu' de Pablo Neruda," Anales de la Universidad de Chile (Santiago), April-June 1956.

_____, "Los versos del capitán," Marcha (Montevideo), May 14, 1954.

_____. "Un viajero de la otra mitad del mundo," Marcha (Montevideo), December 23, 1953.

_____. El viajero inmóvil: introducción a Pablo Neruda. Buenos Aires: Editorial Losada, 1966.

Rokha, Pablo de. "Epitafio a Neruda," Opinión (Santiago), May 22, 1953.

_____. Neruda y yo. Santiago: Editorial Multitud, 1955.

Salama, Roberto. Para una crítica de Pablo Neruda. Buenos Aires: Editorial Cartago, 1957.

Sánchez, Luis Alberto. "Pablo Neruda," Cuadernos Americanos (México) XXI, no. 2 (1962).

Serrano Plaja, Arturo. "Letras: Pablo Neruda," Revista de las Españas (Madrid) no. 102 (1938).

Silva Castro, Raúl. "Notas sobre la juventud literaria en Chile," Claridad (Santiago), July 1923.

_____. Pablo Neruda. Santiago: Editorial Universitaria, 1964.

Suárez-Rivero, Eliana. El gran amor de Pablo Neruda. Madrid: Plaza Mayor, 1971.

180   Bibliography

Subercaseaux, Benjamín. "Las uvas y el viento, " La Nación
(Santiago), March 14, 1954.

Torres-Ríoseco, Arturo. "Neruda y sus detractores, " Cuadernos del Congreso por la Libertad de la Cultura (Paris)
no. 30 (1958).

Vidal, Virginia. "Neruda en el corazón, " Hechos mundiales
(Santiago) no. 60 (November 1972).

Yurkievich, Saúl. "Realidad y poesía (Huidobro, Vallejo y
Neruda), " Humanidades (La Plata) XXXV (1960).

OTHER BOOKS CONSULTED

Alegría, Fernando. Las fronteras del realismo. Santiago:
Zig-Zag, 1962.

_____. Literatura chilena del siglo XX. Santiago: Zig-
Zag, 1962.

_____. Walt Whitman en Hispanoamérica. México:
Colección Studium-5, 1954.

Henríquez Ureña, Pedro. Las corrientes literarias en Hispanoamérica. México: Fondo de Cultura Económica,
1949.

Kayser, Wolfgang. Interpretación y análisis de la obra literaria, 4th ed. rev. Madrid: Editorial Gredos, 1968.

Lukács, Georg. The Meaning of Contemporary Realism. London: Merlin Press, 1962.

_____. Realism in Our Time. New York: Harper & Row,
1964.

Melfi, Domingo. Estudios de literatura chilena. Santiago:
Editorial Nascimento, 1938.

Montes, Hugo, and Julio Orlandi. Historia de la literatura
chilena. Santiago: Editorial del Pacifico, 1955.

Schwartzmann, Felíx. El sentimiento de lo humano en América. Santiago: Universidad de Chile, 1953.

Silva Castro, Raúl. Panorama literario de Chile. Santiago:
   Universidad de Chile, 1961.

Spitzer, Leo. La enumeración caótica en la poesía moderna.
   Buenos Aires: Facultad de Letras y Filosofía, 1945.

INDEX